WILD WHISPERS

TRAVEL ADVENTURES - ANIMAL ENCOUNTERS - CONSERVATION INSIGHTS

Follow your whispers...

GERRY O'BRIEN

To Natty & Bash
Lovely meeting you!
Wishing you many wild adventures :)

Gerry

Ladey Adey Publications

Published: September 2022 Ladey Adey Publications,
Ancaster, Lincolnshire UK

ISBN: 978-1-913579-45-6 (Paperback)

ISBN: 978-1-913579-46-3 (E-Publication)

British Library Cataloguing-in-Publication Data. A catalogue record for this book is available from The British Library.

Cover Design by Ali Bannister.
Proboscis Monkey taken from a photograph by Abbie Wakelin (with permission).
Back Cover Photograph ©Charlie Troman.
Hand drawn illustrations throughout Abigail Simpson

If you enjoyed this book please add a review on Amazon for Gerry.

www.gerryobrienconsultancy.com

Endorsements

Gerry invites you into the magic and beauty of our dwindling biodiversity across the globe, making his book a must-read for conservationists and wildlife lovers everywhere. His adventures provide the perfect base for your imagination to be free; to re-turn and re-connect with the wilds of Nature and the wilderness within you. He reminds you to believe in yourself and to be absolutely authentic to who you are, as I know Gerry to be. After reading this book, you'll set out on your own adventure into wildlife conservation and leave a lasting legacy, like Gerry has, through a heartfelt contribution to Earth's sustainability.

Leah Black, Founder of Ecoinnersense

Wildlife Whispers takes the reader on a delightful journey, as the author's infectious enthusiasm brings alive some of his most memorable animal encounters. A magnificent read for the budding wildlife enthusiast and expert alike!

Sonya Dibbin, Nature Connection Guide at Adore Your Outdoors

Wildlife Whispers is a book written from the heart. Gerry's passion and connection to the natural world is truly inspirational. Interwoven with adventure and exploration is the ever important message of just how precious all life on Planet Earth is.

Faith Douglas, Author of The Nature Remedy

Dedication

Mam and Dad for making the adventures possible.

Abigail for sharing so many magical moments.

Aoife for lighting up my life.

Prelude

'To a man with imagination,
a map is a window to adventure.'

Sir Francis Chichester

This book has been whispering in the back of my mind for years and finally, during lockdown in late 2020, I decided to action it. Once the intention was set, it all started to slot together and it has been a great joy to relive the memories and preserve them in this work.

As a Forest Ranger and Environmental Studies graduate, I am acutely aware of the pressures on the natural world and the biodiversity crisis that we are currently living through. Species are declining faster now than at any time in recorded history. Whilst this book pays brief reference to these pressures, I intentionally chose not to dwell on them.

Instead, I wish to inspire hope. To capture the memories of magical times when my wildlife encounters brought joy and delight to my life. Times when I felt so full with vibrancy, that I glowed with pride for the wonderful diversity of life on this planet. It is my profoundest wish that we not only halt wildlife declines but that we actively reverse them. I believe it is well within our capabilities to do so.

Gerry O'Brien – September 2022

Contents

Foreword

As the Chinese proverb says, *'a journey of a thousand miles begins with a single step'*. Those who read this book will share a great journey with the author – a journey of discovery that took him thousands of miles from Ireland to the forests of South East Asia.

Having reported on the work of the Irish peacekeeping troops in the Middle East for RTE, I can understand the excitement Gerry O'Brien felt when, as a young soldier, he answered the call of peacekeeping in Lebanon. Service in the Middle East was a great experience, but he wanted to see more, so one day he packed it all in and set off in search of new adventures.

It was a journey that took him to the other side of the world and what he saw there reawakened in him a love of wildlife which he and his brother had first encountered in the fields and bogs of his native County Kilkenny. Over the years many readers, now adults, have told me how my books about the fox inspired in them a love of nature, some even embarking on a career in veterinary medicine as a result. As a boy, Gerry read, *Run with the Wind, Run to Earth and Run Swift Run Free.* "I was engrossed," he says, "and they fired my imagination."

Gerry didn't become a vet, but that love of nature which he got from his childhood exploits in the Castlecomer countryside, together with my stories about the fox, stayed with him and was suddenly re-ignited when he went to South East Asia. In the mangroves of Borneo he came face to face with a great diversity of wildlife, including the proboscis monkey and the orangutan, the *'man of the forest who lives and sleeps in the trees'*.

He also came face to face with the heart-breaking realisation that many of these exotic creatures were in danger of extinction because of deforestation.

'When I was a boy,' he recalls, *'there was a harmony with the land and an intuitive feel for the rhythm of nature. But here things had changed. I became truly conscious of humanity's disharmony with the natural world.'*

And so he resolved to devote his working life to protecting wildlife and the environment.

This he does as a Ranger and Educator in the Forest of Dean in England, and he hopes this account of his travels, like my books about the foxes, will awaken in others the need to protect wildlife - not only in the mangroves of Borneo but in this part of the world, too. As the Chinese proverb also says, *'the journey starts beneath one's feet.'* If we look up - the way the author would like us to - we will see the wonderful diversity of wildlife, which is all around us.

Central to his book is a hope that we will enjoy nature and protect it; a hope I heartily endorse.

Tom McCaughren
Author: Run with the Wind

Introduction

Looking back now, I realise how idyllic my childhood days were. Tucked away on the high ground of the Castlecomer Plateau in Ireland's green and rural countryside, I had a perfect base for explorations through the endless fields and local woodland.

Countless hours were spent, relentlessly expanding my horizons on epic adventures. Often accompanied by my brother and cousins, we let our imaginations run riot, creating forts, climbing trees and claiming favourite look out posts over the surrounding landscape.

Frequently, we'd spot Rabbits, Hares and Foxes which always brought a thrill of delight as did the unexpected flushing of pheasants as they exploded out of the coarse grass and hedgerows in front of us.

One memorable day, I had my first bird of prey encounter when a Sparrowhawk flushed a Blackbird out of a nearby copse. I watched enthralled as he pursued with talons outstretched before they frustratingly disappeared from view.

This first raptor sighting drove my excited young mind into overdrive and I was eager to learn more and deepen my understanding of the natural world. I began to trawl through wildlife related literature and became absorbed in books such as *'Watership Down'* by Richard Adams and Tom McCaughren's *'Run with the Wind'* series, where I lost myself imaginatively in animal adventures.

In summer, long days were regularly spent cycling for miles around country lanes and visiting favourite swimming spots in local rivers. We'd pass hours away around the waterside, opening up a whole new world of adventure.

Sometimes in winter we'd return to watch Atlantic Salmon leaping the mini-weirs as they made their way back towards their spawning grounds. I was fascinated by their powerful explosion out of the water and by the enormous journey they'd undertaken from the ocean.

Summer days were also spent helping my father and uncles with traditional turf cutting in the nearby raised bog. In truth, I was often too easily distracted by bog cotton or the sudden discovery of a Frog to be of much use. I'd regularly take opportunities to escape in search of Tadpoles, Water Boatmen, Pond Skaters and Great Diving Beetles in the bog ponds.

Life was simple but happy. Joy was taken in pleasures such as blackberry and strawberry picking, foraging for edible mushrooms and cracking Hazelnut shells open. There was a harmony with the land and an intuitive sense for the rhythm of nature.

My Grand-uncle, lived nearby and he'd sit for hours outside captivating us with stories of Irish folklore and superstition. He imprinted on us a respect for the nature-spirits which also conveniently ensured we got home before sunset, lest we get trapped in a fairy ring.

My parents provided a loving and secure home environment whilst also giving us the freedom to explore naturally and be independent. This unstructured, unsupervised time allowed us to develop our creativity and imagination and to thrive in a pressure free environment. It forged deep cultural values and built up our natural resilience levels.

It was the best playground we could have had and I smile as I reflect on those days. I'm forever grateful to my mam and dad and all the extended family members who helped to facilitate this idyllic time.

As I developed into my late teens, my world started to expand rapidly and I had an incredibly exciting summer, working as a film extra on *Braveheart*, Mel Gibson's action epic, which was being filmed extensively in the Irish Midlands. I also began martial arts training and I obsessively focused on developing physically.

Hours outside were replaced with hours in the gym and self-confidence and esteem developed as my social circle expanded. I loved the feeling of getting fitter and stronger and I gained reasonable success, earning a kickboxing first degree black belt and representing Ireland on many occasions at international tournaments.

By this stage, I had also joined the Irish Defence Forces and ultimately served for five exciting years as an infantry soldier. In addition to extensive weapons and tactical training, I was involved in border duties in Northern Ireland and as an armed guard in Portlaoise Prison.

I qualified as a military driver and drove extensively on cash, prisoner and explosive escorts. I also deployed on three overseas tours as a peacekeeping soldier with the United Nations Interim Force in Lebanon. These were incredibly proud and exciting experiences for me.

Overall, my life was vibrant and adventurous. I was in a committed and happy relationship, was popular and well liked, never shy of social invitations and having sporting and career success. However, whispering away in my mind was an urge to pack it all in and travel the world. Against the advice of close family and friends, I followed those urgings and upon completion of my military contract, I sold everything of value and took off with just a loose travel itinerary in mind. This was when my most transformative life experiences really began...

Re-Awakening

As a young boy, I happened one day upon an image of a curious looking monkey with a large bulbous nose and a ridiculous pot belly. Enthralled by this appearance, I pondered how he was so removed from the lithe and agile presence of other primates. Returning regularly to the image, my imagination spiralled into the life of this bizarre creature in the wild, tropical forests of Borneo.

Years later, as I journeyed the well-trodden backpacker trails of South-east Asia, I nonchalantly picked up a magazine in Kuala Lumpur. Flipping around to its cover, I was struck by a jolt of delighted recognition as the same curious primate stared tantalisingly back at me. I knew instantly where my next travel adventure would take me...

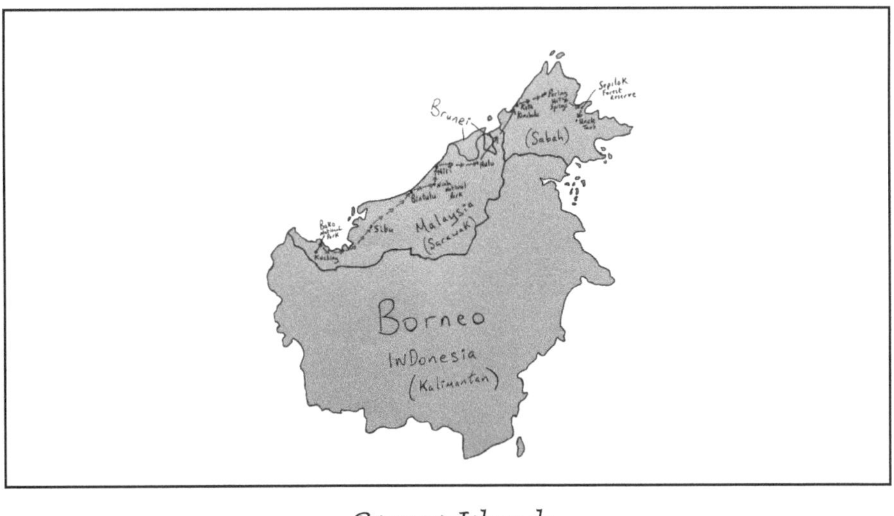

Borneo Island

Bako National Park, Sarawak, Malaysian Borneo. July 2002

Ten minutes into my first trek in the Bornean mangrove forests, I spot the animal I've come to see. Through the branches just slightly overhead, a long grey tail is dangling down, and as I gain better vantage, I notice a curious face, peering through the foliage. An excited thrill ripples through my body as I gaze back at a Proboscis Monkey. I'm mesmerised with a sense of wonder as we share intense moments of absorbing eye contact. The connection is hypnotising. Eventually, the plucky primate breaks the spell and carries on foraging nonchalantly on the leaves. Exchanging smiles with Abigail, my partner and traveling companion, we continue to enjoy his intoxicating presence.

Eventually, we force ourselves onwards with a lightness in step, primed and ready for more wildlife encounters. Over the following hours, we see Long-tailed Macaques in the canopy and a lone Silver Leaf Monkey moving with deliberation through the trees.

We stop regularly to inspect carnivorous Pitcher Plants and occasionally glimpse skinks darting into the undergrowth. We're totally immersed in our surroundings and time slips away quickly. Abruptly, dusk begins to draw in, bringing a sudden realisation that we haven't seen another human for quite some time. Slight anxiety rises as we realise how totally unprepared we are for night time jungle wanderings.

As these thoughts loom, a rapturous commotion suddenly erupts in the canopy ahead and we spot a band of Proboscis monkeys leaping excitedly amongst the trees. They produce alarm calls and it takes a moment to realise that we are the cause of their distress. Females with youngsters attached, vigorously shake branches and throw foliage at us before the dominant male comes prominently into view. He looms large with his huge bulbous nose and protruding pot belly and the intensity of our situation rises as his loud honking alarms resonate across the forest.

My senses tingle! I'm completely overawed by the vibrancy of this wild and primal encounter. We consume his captivating energy as exhilarating moments pass by. Consciously, we then force ourselves onwards to minimise disturbance. As we do so, sprinklings of primate urine rain down from the canopy, encouraging us on our way.

Laughing at the audacity, it feels as if we float the remaining distance back to park HQ, arriving just as darkness closes in.

As we relax in the communal area, Bats swoop on insects attracted by the lights and I take a moment to appreciate our experiences so far. This first trek has already highlighted Borneo's incredible diversity and I can't wait to explore more.

Early next morning we're on the jungle trails once again. Almost instantly we spot Long-tailed Macaques high in the trees ahead and as we come into a forest clearing we encounter a sounder of Bornean Bearded Pigs. Their size and power is incredibly apparent and our adrenalin surges as they charge into the surrounding undergrowth.

We spot the remains of fallen fruit and we realise we have disturbed their feed as Bearded Pigs are renowned for following Macaques to consume the fruit which they drop onto the forest floor. Cautiously continuing onwards, we deliberately stay on the main trail to avoid a flushed encounter with these powerful animals.

Throughout the rest of the morning, we sight more Proboscis Monkeys and glimpse a Flying Lemur. Our senses are on high alert and I regret we haven't extended our park permits to explore further. Regardless, as our

Proboscis Monkey

boat later departs through the mangroves, I feel ecstatic with our incredible experiences.

As if in acknowledgement, a Sea Eagle comes into view, soaring majestically overhead. I smile in gratitude and reflect on the allure of the Proboscis Monkey which encouraged us here. My encounters with this fascinating primate have reawakened my dormant wildlife passion and as I feel its intensity flaring, I already know it is the catalyst for many more wild adventures...

After our exciting visit to Bako, we spend a pleasant few days in the beautiful city of Kuching and also have a wonderful trip to Semenggoh Wildlife Centre, an orangutan sanctuary and nature reserve. Then traveling onwards, we have brief stops at Sibu and Bintulu before visiting Niah National Park to explore its historic caves.

Renowned as one of the world's most important archaeological sites, human remains estimated to be 40,000 years old have been discovered here. We have an atmospheric visit and

I love watching the Cave Swiftlets flying at speed around the vast caverns. An onward journey to Miri then provides an opportunity to get rested and organised before our next wildlife excursion...

Guning Mulu National Park, Sarawak, Malaysian Borneo. July 2002

From our look-out point, we expectantly view the largest cave entrance in the world. We've come to witness a spectacular natural event, the mass exodus of thousands of Bats for their nightly forage. We're excited to be at this famous site, home to at least twelve bat species, with estimates of Wrinkle-lipped Free-tailed Bats alone numbering above three million.

Dusk begins to draw in and we notice the first flight movements around the cave entrance. Swallows and Swiftlets are returning to their cave nests and the first Bats are moving. As light fades further, the emergence intensifies and soon their sheer number becomes all consuming. Many remain high in the sky and disappear into the distance, but others fly low and almost directly overhead to the jungle canopy beyond. I consider the huge volume of prey which sustains this nightly feeding extravaganza and develop a new found appreciation for the abundance of invertebrates in the landscape.

Once the exodus dissipates, we venture on a nocturnal exploration and encounter an Oriental Whip Snake with a green fluorescent coloration. Its forked tongue flicks consistently as it searches for prey and slithers its way amongst the foliage. As it disappears, we venture onwards until we happen upon clusters of flickering lights illuminating the vegetation. Thousands of fireflies are lighting up the black jungle darkness!

This is my first experience of bioluminescence and it's an incredible natural phenomenon to witness. I stand immersed as the insects atmospheric glow shines defiantly against the shadowy dark surrounds. As I marvel at the beauty of the scene and the unfathomable complexity of these fascinating insects, I consider that there's nowhere I'd rather be right now.

Unable to obtain a visa at late notice for Brunei, we instead fly from Mulu to Kota Kinabulu in Sabah. It's a nice city with a friendly vibe and we spend a relaxing few days enjoying simple pleasures like cinema trips and street rambles.

Eventually moving on to Ranau, we have a couple of soothing days at Poring Hot Springs, immersing ourselves in the mineral baths. I desperately want to join an expedition to the top of Mount Kinabulu but due to my lack of robust hiking equipment, I sensibly decide the 4,095 metre summit will be too challenging in the circumstances. It's frustrating but I use the time to learn more about Borneo's unique wildlife and to plan more adventures...

Sepilok Orangutan Rehabilitation Center, Sabah, Malaysian Borneo. July 2002

Borneo is home to the largest arboreal mammal in the world, a Great Ape who lives and sleeps in the trees. Entirely dependent on tropical rainforest for its survival, it is being devastatingly driven towards extinction by excessive rates of deforestation and habitat fragmentation.

This mammal is of course the Orangutan, translating as *'man of the forest'* in the Malay language. Populations have declined so dramatically in recent decades that only remnant groups now remain. Furthermore, as reproduction rates are slow, the loss of a few females can accelerate local extinction rates for viable breeding populations.

Although we're enjoying our travels through Borneo, we are also witnessing the devastating effects of deforestation and becoming increasingly aware of biodiversity declines. It's heart breaking to see and I wish to learn more, so we take a trip to Sepilok to enhance our understanding.

Located on the edge of the Kabili Sepilok Forest Reserve, this unique rehabilitation centre is within 43km of protected forest. It has been established to provide medical care for orphaned, injured and confiscated Orangutans and to rehabilitate individuals towards a wild return. This invaluable work is inspiring to witness as the level of commitment and dedication exuded by staff members is apparent.

For the first time, I begin to seriously comprehend how human actions are causing environmental disharmony and hurtling species towards extinction. It's an uncomfortable feeling as I become truly conscious of humanity's disharmony with the natural world. How can we be so out of balance? I feel a steely resolve hardening and I intuitively feel I'm already being guided towards conservation work.

That afternoon, accompanied by guides, we go deeper into the reserve to search for rehabilitated individuals which have recently returned to the wild. Although their diet is still supplemented with daily feeds, there's no guarantee of sightings as every effort is made to encourage the Apes to forage for themselves. We scan the canopy eagerly hoping for a sighting. As time ticks by, we feel we may miss out and just on the verge of giving up, a sudden clear movement becomes obvious in the canopy ahead.

Descending from a tree above a supplementary feed station, comes an impressively agile adult female. Behind her follows a companion and we stare intently as they settle and eat their fill. It's a heart-warming experience, viewing these great apes in their jungle home. As they eventually climb and swing back into the dense canopy, I visualise a

Bornean Orangutan

time when these magnificent Apes once more thrive in the their tropical home.

Our time in Borneo is running out and after the delights of Sepilok we are eager to finish on a high. We book an expedition to one of South-east Asia's most renowned wildlife hotspots and depart for our jungle camp with excited anticipation...

Uncle Tan's Jungle Camp, Lower Kinabatangan Valley, Sabah, Malaysian Borneo. August 2002

My senses are on high alert as we travel along the Kinabatangan River. With lush tropical forest on both sides, our sightings begin early as a Brahminy Kite soars overhead and a Stork-billed Kingfisher flies low and directly over the water.

In the riverside trees, Long-tailed Macaques are plentiful and an Oriental Pied Hornbill offers a stunning view. We encounter Great Egrets sporadically and then a Grey-headed Fish Eagle takes off from a bare branch perch and flies low across the water with heavy wingbeats. I'm enchanted by its breath-taking enormity.

As we arrive at our jungle camp, we're greeted enthusiastically and then treated to a delicious meal by our friendly and knowledgeable guides. We even meet *Uncle Tan*, the man whose vision has brought eco-tourism opportunities such as this into Sabah (a few months later, we sadly learn he passed away only a short time after our visit. His legacy is well known throughout Sabah and he's posthumously awarded the Certificate of Honour from the Environmental Action Committee for his contributions towards wildlife conservation). Spending time in his company is an incredible honour and it's inspiring to witness first hand his passion for nature. His love and connection to the land resonates deeply with me.

After some rest, we go on a night-time boat safari. The jungle has really come alive now. Buffy Fish Owls are spotted on protruding low-lying branches and Proboscis Monkeys and Macaques are highly active in the riverside canopy. We encounter regular Saltwater Crocodiles and there is trepidation and nervous excitement amongst our group to see this apex predator in such close proximity.

As we cruise by, I vividly recall nature documentary footage of Proboscis Monkeys swimming across rivers to reach prime feeding areas. It's plainly obvious now how risky this strategy is and I silently will the nearby band of primates to stay put. As we eventually make our way back to camp, we spot movement by the riverside and have an incredible view of a Malaysian Civet, an attractively patterned mammal which is largely nocturnal. Its spotted coat and ring banded tail is very distinctive as it slinks amongst the riverside vegetation. It's a fitting end to a rewarding day.

Malaysian Civet

The following morning, an early trek results in sightings of Bornean Bearded Pigs, Pygmy Squirrels, Silver Leaf-Monkeys and a Gliding Lizard. It's a perfect way to start the day and we later relax at camp for rest and respite from the midday heat.

Chatting amicably with our fellow campmates, I am extremely envious of two, who happened upon a huge Bornean Python during their morning walk. Finding the reptile mid-way through it's prey consumption, it was unable to move and our companions captured some unique photographs from a safe and respectful distance. Quite an experience!

In the late afternoon as the heat begins to dissipate, I explore around camp and discover Giant Centipedes and Stick Insects. I also spot a Paradise Fly-catcher and an Oriental Darter perched nearby with its wings held open to dry. I'm on sensory overload and am twitching to get out on night safari once more.

Eventually proceeding to our river boat, Abigail professes her desire to see the elusive Leopard Cat. One of our friendly guides, Tim, laughs and says our chances are almost impossible as in his ten years in the jungle he's only ever had a brief glimpse.

Our exploration that night takes a similar route upriver and we spot a Night Heron and Common Palm Civet to add to our long list of sightings. Then, miraculously, as we round a bend, drinking from the water's edge is a small cat with distinctive leopard spots. Tim turns to face us with an incredulous look on his face and we all bask in the glow that we are experiencing a rare and unique sighting.

As we continue onwards we recognise it will be incredibly hard to beat this experience. However, as we later return towards camp, one of our spotlights locates animal eyeshine in mid-river. We assume Crocodile but as our boat moves closer, there's a collective gasp as we realise it's a Leopard Cat. In its desire to reach the other side, he's taking a dramatic risk with large predators in the vicinity.

Anxious about his vulnerability we draw close and channel this intrepid individual safely to the other side. Safely there, the feline emerges from the water, shakes itself and turns to face the spotlight with an almost quizzical expression. This allows one last lingering view before he disappears into the dense undergrowth. A feeling of awe hangs over our group and we are thankful for our unique experience and his safe crossing. Returning the short distance to camp, I sit in mesmerised silence, processing what has just happened.

Leopard Cat

As we reluctantly begin to decamp the following morning, we suddenly rush into action as word spreads that Pygmy Elephants have been heard nearby. We race to the boats and head downriver, eagerly anticipating an encounter. Stopping periodically, we listen intently but all is quiet. We've missed our opportunity. Nevertheless, we remain full and content with our experiences. The unpredictability of wildlife encounters are what make them so special and just knowing that the jungle is full of constant surprises is exhilarating enough for me.

Deepening

After six months in South-east Asia, our travel funds begin to deplete so we move onwards to Australia to utilise our working holiday visa. Settling initially in Sydney, we gain employment and immerse ourselves in city life. We work hard in the week and then fill our weekends with visits to beautiful beaches and trips to the Blue Mountains and other surrounding National Parks.

I'm fascinated by the unique Australian wildlife and I regularly enjoy the antics of Brush-tailed Possums, Sulphur-crested Cockatoos, and the irrepressible Galah in city parks. It's exciting to have so many vibrant encounters with these alluring species. As the weeks progress, we buy a car and build up our supplies of camping equipment before enjoying the iconic New Year's celebrations at Sydney Harbour to round off an exciting few months.

Sydney to Victoria. January 2003

In early January, we take off with an eager enthusiasm to explore the vast land, making our way initially to Canberra and then onwards into Victoria. On route, we have memorable camping stops in remote nature reserves, enjoying the opportunity to immerse ourselves in the sights and sounds of the Australian bush. We also explore *Ned Kelly* country, visiting locations synonymous with the legendary outlaw. Eventually, we make it to the south coast to an island renowned for a famous wildlife spectacle.

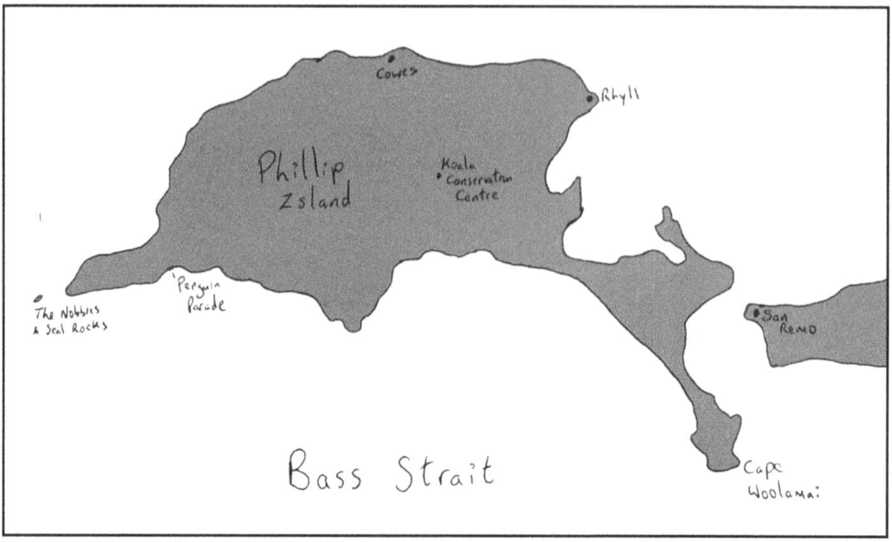

Summerland Beach, Phillip Island, Victoria, Australia

Waiting patiently as the sun begins to set, we scan intently across the tide line, noticing no sign of movement yet. Involuntarily, I shudder as I feel the evening air chill and I wish I'd wrapped up warmer. A gasp of exclamation suddenly brings an air of excitement to our gathered group and necks crane forward in unison as we peer expectantly ahead.

Emerging from the tide, the outline of numerous small creatures become visible. Initially bunching together, they begin to move up the beach with a distinctive waddle, gradually becoming more sharply into focus.

An accompanying ranger commentary outlines exactly what's happening. These are Little Penguins, approximately 30cm tall and they're returning to their beachside burrows after a day hunting for Pilchards and Anchovies at sea. They're following a generational ritual, mirroring the patterns of their ancestors, only now they have a captive human audience.

All thoughts of the chilly evening air dissipate as I witness these little characters waddling distinctively by, intently set on returning to their burrows. They have young to feed. Our vantage point offers a wonderful view and we observe hungry chicks waiting eagerly, their calls getting excitably louder as they reunite with returning adults. I smile as the youngsters greedily consume regurgitated food from their parent's bills. It's nature in its most authentic form and we linger long into the evening as adult birds continue to return and feed their young.

Penguin Waddle ©Phillip Island Nature Parks

Later, as we chat with staff, we realise what an incredible conservation success story this is. Affectionately known as the *Penguin Parade*, viewings are carried out in a strictly non-intrusive manner. Tourism fees directly contribute to species preservation, with the income generated funding vital research such as satellite tracking at sea. In turn, necessary conservation measures are implemented, resulting in increasing populations of Little Penguins nesting on Phillip Island. As I listen to the excited conversations of other audience members that night, I recognise the symbiotic process in action.

The Penguins are helping humans too and the joy and lightness which they bring into our lives is attested to, by the broad smiles all round on this chilly January evening.

Koala Conservation Centre

The following morning, still abuzz with Penguin delight, we visit the Koala Conservation Centre to learn more about this iconic Australian species. It's not an entirely comfortable visit as I become aware of how threatened their populations have become.

Classified as vulnerable on the International Union for Conservation of Nature's (IUCN) Red List, the Koala is recognised as one of the world's most threatened species by climate change. It's sobering to realise that although we're having incredible wildlife adventures, many of the species we encounter are also decreasing in population abundance.

I resolve to learn more about biodiversity declines and the threats which directly impact wildlife. It feels overwhelming but as I witness the dedication, effort and enthusiasm exerted by staff at the conservation centre, I recognise that hope and positivity is extremely powerful too. The fortunes of many species can be turned around with vision and combined efforts to implement focused recovery plans.

Exploring the surrounding woodlands later that day, we have our first sightings of wild Koalas high in the Eucalyptus trees. Although most are snoozing, each sighting brings an exhilarating thrill. There is something quite special about seeing an animal in the wild for the first time and it offers a positive injection to my hardening conservation resolve.

Absorbed by Koalas, we are suddenly taken by surprise when a Short-beaked Echidna ambles out of the bush in front of us. This is our first experience with a monotreme, those bizarre mammals which lay eggs but also feed milk to their young. Known also as the Spiny Ant-eater, due to their covering of spines and taste for ants and termites, we watch this Echidna in full action mode as it uses its strong claws to strip the bark from fallen logs.

We glimpse its sticky tongue working busily as grubs and insect larvae are hungrily found and lapped up. Eventually content, all available food has been found, our spiny friend ambles back into the bush leaving us to absorb another incredible wildlife first.

Echidna

After Phillip Island, we continue southeast along the coastline to a region which is highly recommended. A captivating national park at the southernmost tip of the Australian mainland...

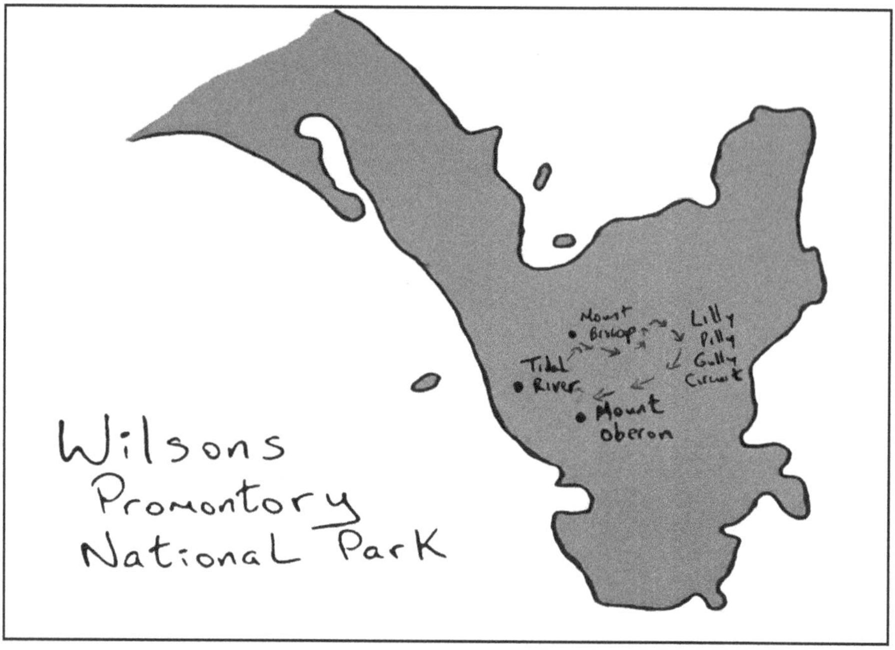

Wilsons Promontory National Park

Wilson's Promontory National Park, Victoria

Setting up camp by picturesque Tidal River, I scan the panoramic landscape. It looks incredibly lush and I'm keen to explore.

Once we've eaten, we take a vigorous hike to the granite summit of Mount Bishop and enjoy views of Bass Strait and the promontory's west coast. Afterwards, we return along the southern slope and descend gradually into the cool temperate rainforest of Lilly Pilly Gully. It's late afternoon by now and although we're in a popular national park, we have the trail to ourselves and we soak up the peace and tranquil solitude of the forest.

As we follow a raised boardwalk section, I'm compelled to stop where the forest opens out. Initially, I look towards the middle distance, but then suddenly become aware of a slight movement in my peripheral vision. Turning slightly, I'm delighted to see a Koala wrapped tightly around a tree trunk, less than ten feet from us. He's snoozing contently and we smile at our incredible proximity. It's brought an extra sprinkling of magic to our afternoon hike.

Koala Huggung a Tree

Returning to the campsite and infused by our experience, I can't quite settle so we take a late evening stroll along the boardwalks through the nearby swamps. I'm startled to see a Common Wombat, tucked cosily on the grass tufts nearby, snoozing contently. I've teased Abigail relentlessly with fake Wombat sightings and now there really is one, she understandably doesn't believe me. Once its presence is confirmed, she's thrilled with another rewarding first on our long list of animal sightings.

Viewing the Wombat from close range, its stocky and powerful body is apparent and it's no surprise when we later read about their renowned burrowing prowess and ability to create extensive underground tunnel systems. As we soak up the last of the evening light on the swamp boardwalk, I feel a deep contentment.

All of these incredible wildlife encounters are enriching our travel adventures and creating lasting memories. There's a lot to be thankful for.

Common Wombat and Joey

Healesville Sanctuary

After our visit to Wilson's Prom, we spend a day at Healesville Sanctuary, a zoo committed to fighting wildlife extinction and specialising in breeding programs and education for native Australian animals. We learn a lot from our time there and are infused with a fresh enthusiasm to spot as many species in the wild as we can.

Throughout our travels, I have got into the habit of researching wildlife hot spots and the species which can be found there. As such, I become aware of an opportunity to spot a particular bird which has intrigued me for a long time.

Kinglake National Park, Victoria

As dawn begins to break, I wake in the back of our car feeling slightly ached and cramped. It takes a moment to register where we are and as remembrance washes over me, I feel a tinge of excitement. We're in Central Victoria, at the southern end of the Great Dividing Range, on a quest to find one of the world's largest songbirds, the Superb Lyrebird. They're noted for their ability to mimic an incredible array of sounds and I'm thrilled at being in their vicinity.

Male Lyrebirds sing loudly as part of a courtship routine to lure females so they can then impress them with an elaborate song and dance routine. This repertoire can include incredible birdsong mimicry but also artificial sounds such as car alarms and chainsaws. Anyone who has seen David Attenborough's famous segment on Lyrebirds in '*The Life of Birds*' cannot fail to be impressed. That's when they first came to my attention and I'm excited now to potentially experience the incredible Lyrebird first-hand.

Eucalypt Forest

Our early morning walk in the Eucalypt Forest is filled with the typical birdsong of the Australian bush and even though we can't distinguish all the species, the distinctive call of the laughing Kookaburra is indisputable and lights up our mood.

As morning progresses, we still have no Lyrebird sightings and I'm beginning to fret our luck may not be in. However, just moments after this thought process, there's an obvious movement through the shrubby ground vegetation. As I turn, I identify the brown plumage of a pheasant sized bird disappearing into the undergrowth. Our first Lyrebird sighting!

Now this is established, I take the self-imposed pressure off and relax more, enjoying the rest of our morning. Over the next couple of hours we spot several more of these fascinating birds skulking through the bush. They're not venturing into the open and we don't get to experience the full range of their vocal repertoire but it's exhilarating nonetheless. It feels rewarding to have put the time and effort in to find this bird for ourselves and our brief encounters have whetted my appetite for further wildlife adventures.

Superb Lyrebird

Periphery

To boost our finances, we work for a couple of weeks on a farm near Shepparton in Northern Victoria. Long days are spent working steadily in the orchard, filling large crates with apples and pears, whilst we wait for an available ferry crossing to Tasmania. When we eventually get an opening, we depart south from mainland Australia across the Bass Strait and it feels like our adventures are taking us to the periphery of the world...

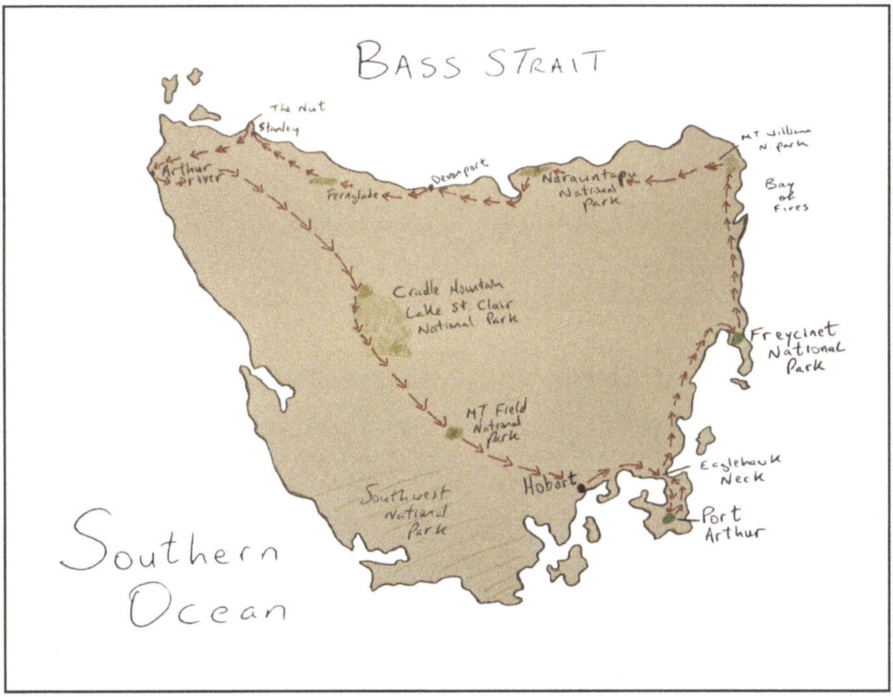

Tasmania

Fernglade Reserve, Tasmania, Australia. February 2003

A tell-tale splash catches our attention and offers our first indication of a possible sighting. We pause patiently, before a second splash heightens our excitement levels and sharpens our focus. We scan the creek intently and get a clear glimpse of a brown furry body, recognising it instantly as the creature we've come to see. To establish a better vantage point, we move cautiously to overhanging rocks, keeping low to mask our presence.

A few moments later a sudden flurry of activity almost directly below us, reveals a definitive view. It's a Platypus, a truly unique creature with a bizarre anatomical mix. We clearly see its duck shaped bill, webbed feet and beaver like tail as it searches the shallows with its distinctive side to side head motion.

By using this movement, the Platypus is utilising electro-receptors in its super sensitive bill to detect bottom-dwelling creatures such as crustaceans, insect larvae and molluscs. It's an incredible thrill to observe, safe in the knowledge we're not causing disturbance.

Spotting a wild Platypus has been an ambition of mine for some time and I think back to a primary school lesson, when a discussion on their bizarre oddity brought our classroom to life. My young imagination was ignited by their image that day and now all these years later, I can't quite believe I'm seeing one in the flesh. It's an almost mythical merging between my boyhood and adult self and as I gaze on the creature; it feels like a moment captured in time.

Platypus

Lying on those rocks, I feel exhilaration. Tasmania feels so *'opposite side of the world'* and our arrival has offered a fresh impetus to our travel adventures, with its lush green freshness providing the perfect recharging tonic.

Buoyed by our Platypus encounter, we enthusiastically continue our explorations and as darkness descends, we arrive at the quaint coastal village of Stanley. In the dark, we can make out the prominent volcanic monolith known as '*The Nut*'.

Overlooking the village, this outcrop is estimated to be 12.5 million years old and juts out prominently into the Bass Strait waters. We tuck up in its atmospheric shadow for a restful sleep.

Rising early the next morning, we walk to its summit to admire the picturesque coastal views. Intuitively, I feel it is a perfect location for raptors and as the thought flashes through my mind, a Peregrine Falcon appears, flying almost directly overhead. It's a vibrant sighting and a reminder to trust my gut feeling. I recognise that the more time I'm spending immersed in nature, the stronger my intuition feels, which in turn is leading to many magical wildlife encounters.

Later, we take a long drive to the Arthur-Pieman Conservation Area, known affectionately as the *'Edge of the World'*. Travelling for miles into the remote region, we eventually park close to a particularly wild and desolate beach.

Taking a refreshing walk, we witness the enormous Southern Ocean waves thundering in against the rugged coastline. Scanning the seaward horizon, it's sobering to contemplate that the next land due west is South America, almost 7000 miles away. It seems as if we're on the periphery of the world as we embrace the raw and powerful atmosphere. As I inhale the fresh ocean air, I'm infused with excitement and begin to formulate plans for our next Tasmanian adventure...

Cradle Mountain/Lake St Clair National Park, Tasmanian Wilderness World Heritage Area. February 2003

Walking around Dove Lake, I can't help but regularly pause to absorb our iconic surroundings. The recognisable dolerite peak of Cradle Mountain looms ahead, offering a prominent reminder of our location within the pristine Tasmanian wilderness.

As we loop around the lake, the mountain continues to hold my eye and I feel an almost magnetic pull drawing us forward until we eventually pass beneath its summit, into an area of cool temperate rainforest.

We gradually arc back towards park HQ, passing by many magnificent King Billy Pines on the way. These ancient specimens are perfectly attuned to this tough environment and are estimated to live for over 1000 years.

After lunch we take a second walk to Cradle Lake and Wombat Pool, spotting endemic Pandani Plants on the way. We're highly charged by the pristine environment and as darkness closes in, we return, reinvigorated to our campsite. It's a cold night and the temptation to tuck up early is overtaken by a desire to spot Tasmania's most famous inhabitant.

I begin to explore earnestly and before even leaving the camping area I spot a small dog like creature moving steadily in my direction. I freeze, remaining resolutely still and get rewarded with an intrepid Tasmanian Devil passing nonchalantly by. Renowned as notable scavengers, I assume this fellow is on the prowl for food but the boldness and clear intent makes me reconsider.

I recall an earlier conversation with a park ranger who mentioned the Devils are notorious for stealing camping equipment and clothing left carelessly lying around. Footwear, towels and socks are particular favourites and are utilised regularly as den accessories.

As I watch this purposeful character stalking the campsite, I chuckle at the notion of someone's favourite trainer being snatched away. I'm glad we've tucked all our belongings safely inside our tent!

The following day, we visit Lake St Clair, Australia's deepest lake. As we round a bend, I spot the loping run of another Devil as it disappears quickly into the undergrowth. With it being a largely nocturnal creature, I hadn't anticipated the sighting and I'm elated with the thrill of the surprise encounter.

Tasmanian Devil

Later, as we relax by the lakeside, we contemplate how nice it would be to hike the famous overland track which connects Cradle Mountain to Lake St Clair. We also discuss the Thylacine, popularly known as the Tasmanian Tiger due to its distinctive stripes. Tragically driven to extinction through excessive human pressures, the last known specimen died in 1936.

However, over the years there have been numerous unverified reports of their continued existence. We marvel at the wondrous possibility that somewhere in the vast Tasmanian wilderness, the Thylacine is still roaming. Unrealistic perhaps, but it's uplifting to consider that perhaps humans haven't complete dominion over the land.

Later that evening on the fringes of our campsite, we have the good fortune to see a Spotted-tailed Quoll. This carnivorous marsupial is an incredibly adept predator, preying on mammals such as Possums, Gliders and

Rabbits but is also known to eat carrion, as well as birds and their eggs. As a primarily nocturnal, solitary creature, we're incredibly lucky to get such a good sighting. One of the ranger team tells us this particular Quoll has been seen regularly around the campsite. They are concerned it may be injured and have tried to capture it for some time. Not an easy task!

Traveling onwards, we visit Mount Field National Park and enjoy a walk to one of Tasmania's most cherished places, the breath-taking Russell Falls. Relishing the incredible lushness of the deep green forest, we pass by towering swamp gum trees before enjoying the beauty of the fall's multi-level water cascades. In the afternoon, we also visit Horseshoe Falls and Lady Barron Falls before setting up camp by the banks of the River Tyenna.

Spotted-Tail Quoll

That night, we return towards Russell Falls and observe the multiple bright gleams of Glow Worms standing out starkly against the forest vegetation. Upon reaching the falls, we stand in the moonlight and reflect on our time in the Tasmanian Wilderness. We've only seen a fraction of the accessible locations but it's given us a flavour of the broader region. I hope someday to return and explore more of this fascinating land.

After Mount Field, we enjoy a pleasant few days in Hobart and then move on to the famous preserved convict site at Port Arthur. Soaking up its history, we enjoy an atmospheric late evening ghost tour and later are lucky enough to spot two Southern Brown Bandicoots at our campsite. These nocturnal marsupials with their short stocky bodies, pointed snout and rounded ears are a really exciting find.

We also visit Remarkable Cave in Tasman National Park and explore the wonder of the tessellated pavement at Eaglehawk Neck. As we head up the east coast, we experience stunning Wineglass Bay in Freycinet National Park and have our first encounters with Bennett's Wallabies. Known also as the Red-necked Wallaby, this species is regularly found in coastal scrub habitat.

Sightings of Tasmanian Pademelons also bring delight. They're easily distinguished from the Wallabies by their small squat size and are predominantly nocturnal and shy which makes them more difficult to find. It's impossible not to be enamoured by their cuteness.

During my nightly explorations, I'm fortunate to encounter a White-lipped Snake and also to have another marvellous Echidna sighting. Considering our schedule, we've crammed a lot into our Tasmanian explorations and we're sad as we reach our final day. Nevertheless, there's time for one more adventure...

Tasmanian Pademelon

Narawntapu National Park, Tasmania. March 2003

Setting up camp in the early evening, it's apparent we're the only overnight visitors in this unique coastal habitat. It is understandable, considering the biting chill in the air. Wrapped up warm, we feel excited for the opportunity to experience another wildlife rich location. As we explore in earnest, we move through the coastal heathlands towards Bakers Beach. Time passes quickly and once dusk looms, we loop back towards our camping area, where we're greeted by the sight of countless grazing marsupials. Large numbers of Forester's Kangaroos, Bennett's Wallabies and Tasmanian Pademelons are all in plain sight on the open grassland. It's a prime feeding area and the lack of humans has encouraged these large numbers to gather. As we gaze, it's easy to differentiate the three species with the Pademelons especially standing out, their small squat bodies looking tiny next to the Kangaroos and Wallabies.

Settling down for the night, I later awake in the early hours and struggle to get back to sleep. The longer I lay there, the colder I feel, so I utilise my military mindset and decide to get outside to get my blood circulation pumping and warm up.

As I unzip the tent, I'm astounded to see vast numbers of animals grazing in close proximity. Kangaroos, Wallabies and Pademelons still in abundance, but now surrounding our tent, their silhouettes standing out sharply in the moonlight. As I step out, they initially move back but then gradually settle and grow accustomed to my presence. I sit quietly whilst they contently feed and once I feel they've adjusted to me, I quietly complete some press ups to warm up. Then, as I sit still, in the glow of the full moon, the peaceful grazers gradually move closer and closer until I am completed surrounded.

Their presence is serene. I smile contently and soak up the enchanting scene. It's a meaningful natural connection and I'm hesitant to go back inside the tent. Sitting in the cold for as long as I can, I consume the marsupial magic. It feels like the perfect way to end our Tasmanian adventure.

Progression

Upon return from Tasmania, we enjoy a change in atmosphere, spending a few days soaking up the big city vibe in Melbourne and catching up with travel friends. We relax at our campsite in Coburg, attend the local gym, browse around shopping malls and visit Ramsey Street, the fictional cul-de-sac from the Australian soap opera, Neighbours. We also embrace the atmosphere at the Old Melbourne Gaol and attend the Formula 1 Grand Prix which offers a contrasting experience to our wildlife adventures. Overall, it's a lovely time and sets us up nicely for further progress across the vast Australian continent...

Cape Bridgewater, Victoria. 13th March 2003

As we enjoy the spectacular coastal scenery of the Great Ocean Road, we happen upon an opportunity to visit the largest mainland colony of Seals in Australia. The chance to observe hundreds of Australian and Long-nosed Fur Seals from the water is too good to miss and before we know it we're on a small charter boat heading towards the colony. We're assured by the strict guidance regulations which the business operates under, and as we approach closer the sights and sounds of Seals begin to dominate.

Our excitement levels ramp up as we flit our attention between the individuals on the rocks and others in the surrounding water. As the skipper cuts the engine, we gently bob along and I begin to focus on specific characters.

One enquiring fellow pops his head out of the water directly alongside and stares curiously right at me. I return his gaze, losing myself in the depths of his large round dark eyes and peaceful persona. The numbers of Seals begin to intensify and their playful and curious energy is palpable. It's as if they're encouraging us into the water but this is not possible due to conservation restrictions and the regular presence of Great White Sharks in the area.

As we continue to bob gently along, large adult bulls study us from rocky platforms and their cacophony of barks, grunts and honks reverberate around us. I'm enthralled by their natural symphony and the magic of the experience.

We idle into a nearby cave, where more Seals peer at us from rocky ledges, their vocalisations echoing atmospherically. It's raw and emotive and I can't stop smiling. Yet all too soon our time is done and we return to the jetty, with a warm internal glow. We have experienced the purity of nature in a most vibrant and wondrous way.

Upon reaching shore, we take a short walk around the headland to view the Seals from a different perspective on the cliff top. On the way, a sudden ground movement catches my attention. With a start, I recognise a Lowland Copperhead Snake, it's mid-brown to yellowish scales glinting beautifully in the sun. It slithers away peacefully into the nearby scrub and I gleefully consider the wondrous wildlife yet to discover in this vast land.

Later, heading towards Adelaide for St Patrick's Day festivities, our plans undergo a change when an opportunity for an impromptu adventure pops up...

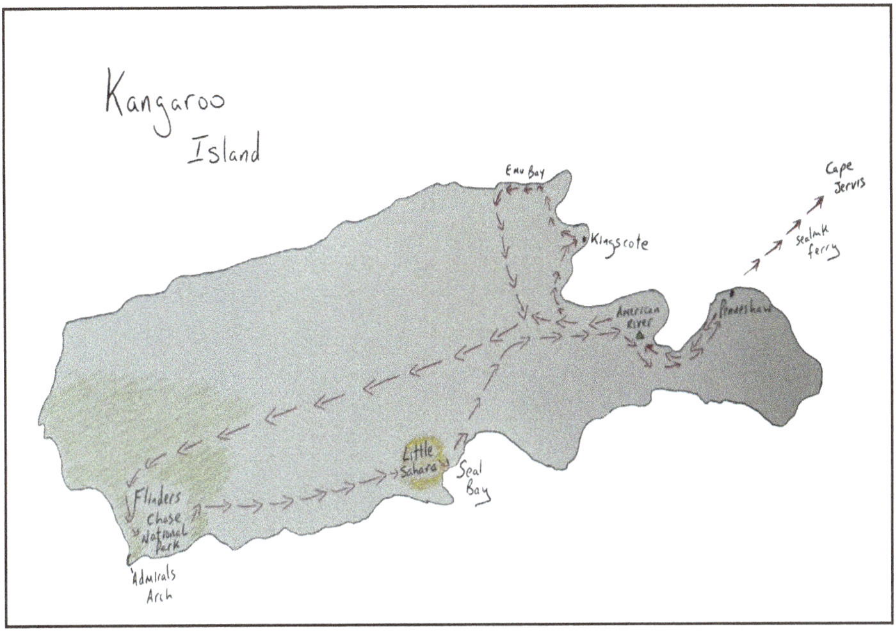

Kangaroo Island

Kangaroo Island, South Australia.
17th March 2003

It's St Patrick's Day and as far as I know, I'm the only Irish person on the island. Having arrived the previous day, we've already enjoyed a drive on the beach at Emu Bay and watched the Pelicans being fed at the pier in Kingscote.

We've also spotted Koalas, Yellow-billed Spoonbills and Wedge-tailed Eagles but today I'm feeling nostalgic and sensing the distance from home. I'm used to being away for long periods but on this morning, I'm feeling a strong pang for family and friends. Eager to keep my mind occupied, I plan our explorations for the day ahead and we soon find ourselves in Flinders Chase National Park in the Island's south-west corner.

We visit the impressive cluster of granite boulders known as Remarkable Rocks and marvel at how they've been formed by the forces of nature over five hundred million years. Soaking up the tranquil atmosphere, we enjoy the views over the nearby Casuarina Islets. It's a wonderful location to relax and I feel at peace as I enjoy the sunlight on my face.

Gerry at Remarkable Rocks

Abigail at Remarkable Rocks

Eventually, we move onwards to another nearby landmark, Admirals Arch. Spending some time at the viewing platform, we watch the Long-nosed Fur Seal colony below, lingering until hunger entices us back to our car.

As we prepare lunch, I'm bemused by the roguish behaviour of Kangaroo Island Kangaroos trying to help themselves to the food in our open car boot.

Hungry Kangaroo Island Kangaroos

This unique sub-species of the Western Grey Kangaroo is not found on the Australian mainland and it's quite a novel experience to share our dining time with them. Tammar Wallabies are present too, as are Scarlet Robins, the superbly colourful red breasts of the males, standing strikingly out against the shrubby foliage.

After lunch we explore the surrounding area on foot and encounter our first Heath Monitor also known as the Rosenberg's Goanna. It's explosive speed up the sand dunes is an exhilarating sight and I race in pursuit as it disappears quickly over the top. By the time I get there, its long gone and my excitement is tinged with a mild disappointment that I've not had a more prolonged encounter. Over the course of the next hour, I scour the surrounding area in hope of another sighting.

Heath Monitor

Just as I'm on the verge of giving up, another large Monitor races across an opening directly in front, providing an excellent viewing. My perseverance has paid off! Eventually content, I return to our car to head east for our next wildlife escapade.

Seal Bay, Kangaroo Island, South Australia

Arriving at Seal Bay, we book on a late afternoon tour to see the resident Australian Sea Lions. As the world's rarest Sea Lion species, it's an amazing opportunity to learn more about them. Our enthusiastic and knowledgeable guide takes us close to the heart of the colony and points out their noticeable differences compared to Seals. The most distinctive and obvious contrast is the Sea Lion's ability to 'walk' on land using their large flippers, as opposed to a Seal's belly wriggle across ground. External ear flaps on the Sea Lions are also pointed out as a distinguishing feature.

Australian Sea Lion

We feel privileged to have such an illuminating tour and afterwards we meander back along the boardwalk to a viewing platform overlooking the colony. I smile as I notice some of the Sea Lions raising a flipper to the cool breeze. We've learned this is their effective strategy against overheating.

Overlooking the sprawling ocean, it's fascinating to consider that these animals have been an integral part of this coastline for thousands of years. It's been wonderful to share a couple of hours in their company.

Energised by this experience, we take a final late evening exploration around Little Sahara, a system of huge coastal sand dunes located nearby. Formed over 7000 years, the dunes vary in size with some up to 70 metres above sea level.

As I traverse across them, it's easy to imagine I'm in the depths of the Sahara Desert as it's so atmospheric. When we eventually return to our remote campsite, I realise I haven't felt homesick since my early morning pondering. My time exploring the wild reaches of Kangaroo Island has been the perfect tonic and a unique way to celebrate St Patrick's Day.

Once back on the mainland, we progress westward across the vast expanses of the Nullarbor Plain. We have the road more or less to ourselves, aside from the occasional road train passing in the opposite direction. These huge freight trucks are an impressive sight but I prefer the moments of stillness when we have the long miles to ourselves.

We regularly stop by the roadside so we have time to properly absorb the scale of the landscape and as ever we're on constant alert for wildlife.

We frequently see Wedge-tailed Eagles, each sighting giving us an exhilarating thrill. These birds are huge and throughout our journey, we encounter many feeding on carrion by the roadside. As we close in on approach, they

Wedge-tailed Eagle

take off with slow powerful wingbeats, allowing us a close proximity viewing.

Sometimes we pause to watch them soaring effortlessly on the thermals overhead and we consider how large their territories must be.

We also spot our first wild Dingo and encounter Western Grey Kangaroos. Occasionally, we even glimpse large Red Kangaroos in the distance. Journeying across the endless miles is quite an experience and allows us to truly comprehend the vastness of the land.

Once across the Nullarbor, we explore the beautiful South-west region of Western Australia before eventually arriving in Perth where we enjoy a welcome break at my Uncle Tom's house. After months on the road, it's so nice to enjoy home luxuries and the comforting presence of relatives. We're looked after extremely well and appreciate the opportunity to meet members of my extended family.

Nullarbor Roadsigns

I chat often with Tom about his younger days in Ireland, his life in Australia and his service as a UN soldier in the Congo in the 1960's. It's great to have this quality restful time and it freshens us up nicely for our next big distance push up the coast.

As we travel north from Perth, we explore the breath-taking Pinnacle Desert at Nambung National Park, where thousands of limestone pillars are scattered across the yellow sand landscape. We linger for quite a while, observing the colour change and lengthening shadows as the sun sets. Then in the full moon light we walk around the pinnacle formations again, absorbing the serene and tranquil atmosphere.

Further north we view Stromatolites at Lake Thesis. These remarkable living fossils have produced oxygen for about 3.5 billion years and are amongst the oldest living organisms on earth. It's extraordinary to consider their life span and as we arrive at Shark Bay we have an opportunity to see them again…

Shark Bay World Heritage Area, Coral Coast, Western Australia. 19th April 2003

As we view the Stromatolites from the purpose built boardwalk at Hamelin Pool, I visualise how life on the planet once looked. I find myself mentally scanning through the phases of history and acknowledge my luck at living in this time where life is generally pleasant.

Shark Bay

There has never been as much opportunity to explore the planet and with this thought in mind, we pay a visit to Shell Beach, a fascinating area made up entirely of billions of small shells.

We enjoy a swim in the crystal clear waters before drying off and contemplating how bizarre this anomaly is.

The shells underfoot are estimated to be up to ten metres deep and stretch for over 70 kilometres along the coastline. It's an unusual sensation as we walk barefoot along them.

Later stopping at Eagle Bluff, we search for Sharks, Rays, Dolphins and Dugongs from the cliff top but unfortunately don't spot any. Then arriving at Monkey Mia, we experience the magnificent Bottlenose Dolphins who are renowned for their daily visits to shore.

Under the watchful eye of Parks and Wildlife Officers we stand quietly on the tide line and allow the Dolphins to approach closely.

Bottlenose Dolphin at Monkey Mia

Incredibly, a mother and calf come within a few feet and we listen respectfully as the officers outline the guidelines which ensure their wild behaviour is not altered.

Dolphins have visited the shallows of Monkey Mia for over fifty years and we feel hugely privileged to witness this wonderful wildlife spectacle. Through the mid-day heat, we then sit in the theatrette and watch episodes of *Blue Planet*. As it begins to cool in the late afternoon, we embark on a catamaran cruise in the marine park.

We spot more Dolphins and a couple of Loggerhead Turtles as they come to the surface for air. We also get a glimpse of a Dugong as it moves slowly beneath the shallow waters. Known affectionately as *Sea Cows* for their peaceful grazing on marine grasses, Dugongs are found in coastal waters of the Indian and Western Pacific Oceans and I'm super excited to see one.

Dugong

We return to shore, as the sun begins to set and enjoy watching the Australian Pelicans being fed on the beach. It's delightful to see their huge bills opening wide as they swallow down large quantities of fish. It feels like a fitting end to a perfect day on Australia's Coral Coast.

Pelicans at Monkey Mia

Giants

Continuing north up the coastline, we cross the Tropic of Capricorn and arrive at Exmouth, a coastal town near the top of the North West Cape. This brings an air of excitement as we know our time here offers the possibility of swimming alongside an ocean giant...

Ningaloo Reef, Western Australia. April 2003

"*We've got an Orca ahead!*" This unexpected announcement sends a rippled buzz of excitement through our dive boat. We're searching for Whale Sharks in the clear waters of the Indian Ocean, so this encounter with an Orca brings incredulous disbelief. A palpable buzz overtakes the boat and as we draw closer, the first sighting of distinctive black and white colouration brings a collective outpouring of emotion.

Just as we reach prime viewing range, the huge mammal disappears beneath the surface, leaving a lingering silence hanging in the air. Seconds pass by and all remains still. There's a palpable tension beginning to mount when a sudden explosive breach directly alongside brings an outpouring of joy.

We have a stunning view of the animals enormity before it disappears into the deep once more. A feeling of reverence overcomes us and within moments there's another breach, this time directly in front of us. Our proximity is incredible and we're in awe at the raw brute power on display.

This is an animal perfectly in tune with its environment, leaving us in no doubt of its formidable capabilities.

Our Captain surmises that the lone individual is most likely a transient male juvenile. Although generally highly social creatures, it's not unusual for a male Orca to leave its mother and travel alone for a period of time. Whatever its story, we're thankful for our magical encounter as he continues to charm us with his presence. It feels like there's a bewitchment in the air and I'm intensely tuned into my surroundings like never before. I savour the unique moment and wish I could contain it forever. Gradually, the exhilaration begins to fade and is replaced by a sense of contentment as our ocean giant eventually departs. Watching him go, I feel thankful for the gift he has bestowed upon us this day.

Orca

Prior to this incredible encounter, we've already had an amazing time on the reef. During our scuba dives we've spotted graceful Eagle Rays and huge Potato Cod and we've also had a mixed pod of Common and Spinner Dolphins, energetically bow riding in front of our boat. It's been an incredible experience and as we return to land we have the warm glow and contented feeling of a day well lived.

The next few days are spent in blissful relaxation as we enjoy the atmosphere of the Whale Shark Festival in town. This annual event brings the community together in celebration of the animal which brings so much joy and prosperity to the region. We enjoy chatting, sharing stories and having social nights out with other adventurous souls.

During this time, we also take the opportunity to dive at the world famous Navy Pier which has been voted as one of the top ten dive sites in Australia. Used only occasionally by the Navy and out of bounds to the general public, it can only be dived through a licensed company in times of slack tides, as the currents are so strong. This lack of regular disturbance allows for an incredible diversity of marine life and we're treated to a visual feast of colourful soft corals and sponges as well as sightings of Reef Sharks, Wobbegongs and Moray Eels. We also see Grouper, Snapper and Butterfly, Angel and Parrot Fish. It's a spectacular experience and we feel Navy Piers reputation as a pristine dive site is well justified.

A couple of days later, we're back on the ocean once more in search of Whale Sharks. We know a spotter plane is at work overhead so we relax and focus on enjoying our day, regardless of the outcome. Internally however, it's obvious we're craving another magical encounter. By mid-morning a call comes through... a Whale Shark has been spotted nearby! Giddy excitement ensues as we don our wet suits, flippers, goggles and snorkel. We have strict instructions not to approach the Shark and to leave a three metre exclusion zone. Once positioned, everyone excitedly dives into the ocean and as the last one in I almost immediately became disorientated. I lose sight of my dive mates and as I struggle to get my bearings, a clear thought passes through my mind '*Where's the Shark?*'

The next few moments are perhaps the most surreal and exhilarating of my life. A strong intuitive impulse urges me to turn and as I do so, a huge mouth looms suddenly out of the blue. Never have I felt so small and out of control as I do in that moment, yet time seems to slow and I'm engulfed by a curiously strange peace as the huge creature approaches and gently nuzzles me.

I'm mesmerised by its sheer size and intricate beauty and it too seems intrigued by my presence. We share a magical moment of connection before my conscious mind fires back into life and I recall the clearly defined dive brief.

I suddenly feel anxious about a reprimand from my dive instructor so I swim sideways and the immense shark follows briefly, nuzzling at my flippers. It then continues forward and I gaze in awe as the full enormity of its spotted body length passes by, before once more disappearing into the blue.

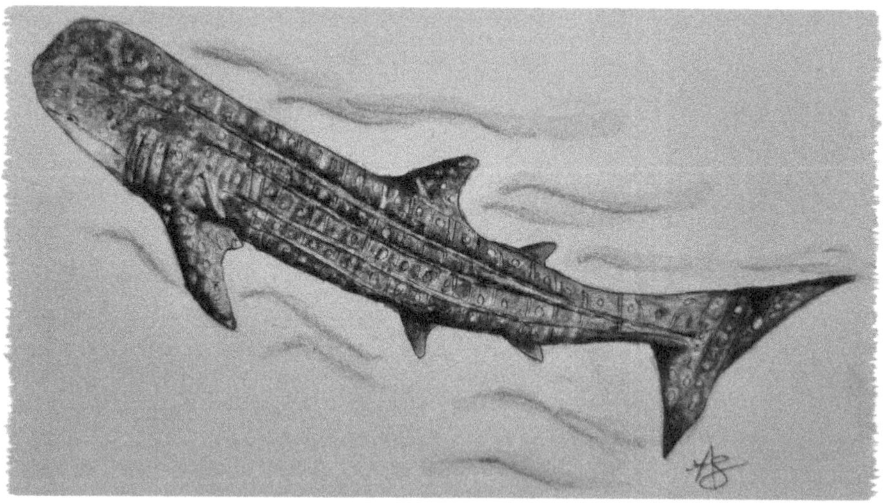

Whale Shark

Lingering in the water in the immediate aftermath, I suddenly become aware of one of the dive instructors nearby. She's pointing vigorously downwards. My eyes follow her signal and deep below us I'm startled to see two Minke Whales swimming side by side. Another giant encounter, it's almost too much to absorb in the moment. Eventually, as we emerge back onto our dive boat, we sit in enraptured silence as we process the magic of our experiences.

My fears at being told off are quickly dispelled as the instructor gives a friendly, "*He liked you!*" acknowledgement. The Shark after all had approached me and I feel incredibly fortunate to have had this intimate and personal encounter. I know it will remain etched in my mind for the rest of my days.

At our campsite that evening, I sit quietly with a cold beer to absorb the excitement of the day. Totally unannounced, five Emus suddenly appear in my peripheral vision. I sit in stunned silence as they saunter nonchalantly closer. They're searching the ground intently for morsels of food and seem totally unperturbed by my presence. Occasionally looking in my direction, they advance to within a few feet before continuing on their way.

Up close, their size is daunting and I'm in total awe of these massive birds. I realise it's an adult male with juveniles, as the male Emu takes responsibility for raising the young. I smile broadly as they disperse across the campsite and acknowledge my luck at having another intimate giant encounter to round off the day.

Emu

Immersion

After Ningaloo, we explore the diverse gorges of Karijini National Park. By day we scramble through ancient rocky chasms and dip in crystal clear waterways and at night we relax around a campfire and marvel at the incredible night sky. It's an idyllic time and makes us feel like proper explorers.

Later we continue north, and settle in Broome for a few days where we enjoy the laid back ambiance and treat ourselves to an atmospheric sunset Camel ride through the sand dunes at Cable Beach. We're having the time of our lives but there's an underlying anxiety that our travel funds are running low.

Knowing we have to find work soon, we continue east across the Kimberley, passing through Fitzroy Crossing and Halls Creek. It feels good to have the open road in front of us and to have a renewed sense of purpose.

The day slips away quickly as the miles pass by and darkness looms suddenly, catching us by surprise. We're not quite ready to stop so we continue driving into the night on the remote outback roads. It's a rookie mistake.

Our headlights seem paltry against the black dark and Kangaroos and Wallabies appear at the last moment as they bounce in panic in front of us. It's highly stressful and I reduce speed dramatically to avoid a collision. Stunned by their abundance, I keep my concentration levels high as we crawl along at minimal speed, until eventually reaching the roadhouse at Turkey Creek, 879 kilometres from Broome.

We pull in, with relief, to a broad parking area and settle down for the night in the back of our car. We're soundly asleep within moments.

Early next morning, we treat ourselves to a tasty breakfast at the roadhouse and notice a sign offering helicopter flights through the canyons at Purnululu National Park, known affectionately as the Bungle Bungles. Given our situation, we haven't the time or resources to properly explore this vast region and we realise it's our only opportunity to get a feel for the area. We decide to forget about money and enjoy the experience. It's a good decision. Our flight through the canyons is exhilarating and feels otherworldly as we weave through the narrow gorges and around the unique beehive shaped sandstone domes. It's an incredibly memorable experience.

Afterwards we journey onwards and arrive at a town close to the Northern Territory border. It's make or break time as we

Purnululu National Park - The Bungle Bungles

know we have to find work here in order for our adventures to continue...

Kununurra, Western Australia. May 2003

Stretching upright to offer respite to my aching back, I stare intently ahead. A heat haze shimmers over the field. Wiping the sweat from my brow, I bend once more with a wry grimace and resume slowly inching forward, thinning out corn stalks as I go.

It's an incredibly tough graft in 43°C heat, but it feels good to put in a hard-working shift and I embrace the discomfort by focusing on the newness of my surrounds. It's good to be earning again and my hard work on the corn field pays off leading to a job at a local smallholding Banana Farm.

Over the following weeks, I fall into a comfortable routine and on my dawn journeys to work, I regularly spot Southern Boobook Owls perched on roadside branches and occasionally see a Tawny Frogmouth silhouetted prominently in the early morning light. I love this morning journey and it's an exciting and adventurous start to the day. Once on the farm, work is hard, but enjoyable too, and I consistently keep my wildlife radar on high alert, encountering Skinks and Lizards on a regular basis.

One late evening as I travel home after overtime, a huge Water Python slithers in front of me, its enormous length practically covering the entire road width. I estimate it's well over two metres in length. It's fascinating to acknowledge that snakes of this size are in my living and working environment.

Abigail sources work at the local school and we move as tenants into a lovely house which is provided for us. We feel properly embedded within the community and have regular invites to BBQs and local football games. It's such a blissful time.

One of our highlights is a boat trip along the Lower Ord River with friends. As we traverse remote stretches of the scenic waterway, we spot Fresh and Saltwater Crocodiles and are also astounded to see Bull Sharks thrashing in the water. I hadn't realised these powerful sharks travel so far upriver and its sobering to see them in such close proximity.

We also encounter Archerfish, an amazing species which target overhead insects with squirts of water from their mouth and we witness this extraordinary hunting strategy first hand. The diversity of bird life is incredible and we log sightings of; Australian Darters, Sacred Kingfishers, Little Pied Cormorants, Intermediate Egrets, Eurasian Coots, Rainbow Bee-eaters, Mistletoe Birds, Rufous Night Herons and Great Bower Birds. Overall, it's an exhilarating day, providing us with a warm glow and another lasting memory.

A short time afterwards, we take advantage of a work break and embark on our first trip into the Northern Territory. Stopping at Victoria River Roadhouse, we're delighted to see our first Blue-winged Kookaburras, perching prominently close to the car park. Inside, we have a lovely surprise when we meet a travel friend whom we met in Exmouth.

We share a meal and pass a pleasant couple of hours reminiscing. However, once back at our car, our mood changes when it fails to start. We're faced with a dilemma and it seems we'll have to stay at the roadhouse overnight until a mechanic is available. It's 200 kilometres to Katherine, the next town. Later on, before we prepare to bed down, I turn the key once more and the engine suddenly fires into life. Feeling exuberant, we commit ourselves and travel at 50kph until our car eventually stalls about ten kilometres short of Katherine. It's dark now and our engine is steaming so we pop the bonnet to allow it to cool off before settling down so we can face the situation fresh in the morning.

A loud early morning rapping on our window wakes us with a start. A passer-by has come to offer assistance. He's a mechanic by trade and with oil, water and a lot of coaxing, we eventually manage to get our trusty Subaru revived. Spluttering our way to the nearest garage, we get confirmation that our engine is finished. It'll cost $1600 for a new one. We take time to clear our heads and decide it's not worth the payment for a couple of months use.

We've already travelled over 20,000 kilometres from Sydney, through six states and now into the Northern Territory. We've more than had our monies worth and it's time to cut our losses and move on. The garage pay us $150 to take it off our hands and within the hour, we've continuing onwards in a luxury hired car to enjoy our holiday in style. It's quite liberating and I feel relieved at how the situation has worked out.

Stopping off at Litchfield National Park to recharge ourselves, we spend time marvelling at huge termite mounds which amazingly are all aligned in a north-south direction. We take a lovely walk to Florence Falls and have a beautiful dip in the plunge pool, surrounded by lush rainforest. It's

Gerry with his Trusty Suburu

wonderfully refreshing. Settling at Wangi Falls Campsite for the night, we enjoy another walk and refreshing dip the following morning. We feel completely free and all thoughts of car trouble have long dissipated from our minds.

We travel onwards to Darwin and explore for a couple of days before heading towards Kakadu National Park, a region I've always been keen to visit. On the way, we have an opportunity (too good to resist) to stop at the township of Humpty Doo for a couple of amusing photographs. Not long afterwards we find ourselves in the Adelaide River catchment, home to vast numbers of Saltwater Crocodiles.

Before we know it, we're travelling down river on the famous Jumping Croc Cruise to learn about the importance of Crocodiles to their ecosystem. It's a beneficial trip and we have incredible up-close sightings as Crocs explode out of the water to feed on the provided Buffalo meat. A White-bellied Sea Eagle also swoops low in front of our boat and Whistling Kites sporadically dive bomb from overhead. It's another exhilarating wildlife experience, providing a natural high whilst also developing our knowledge and

Saltwater Crocodile

understanding of these animals.

Further on at the Window on the Wetlands Information Centre, we spot our first Jabiru, a large member of the Stork family. We're also surprised to see enormous Water Buffalo. Not originally native to Australia, but imported in the 19th Century as a source of meat for remote settlements. Over time, the Buffalo were abandoned and are now feral and widespread across large sections of Northern Australia. As an introduced species, they cause significant damage to native wetlands although they also provide a source of high quality food for resident Saltwater Crocodiles.

Kakadu National Park, Northern Territory. 8th July 2003

Eventually we arrive at Kakadu National Park and stop off at Mamukala Wetlands to observe the vast array of birdlife. Flocks of Magpie Geese fill the waterways and as we take a gentle walk, we also spot Plumed Whistling Ducks, Comb-crested Jacanas and Jabirus. I'm familiar with Jacanas from seeing them in Kununurra and I chuckle as I watch this delicate little wader skimming across the lily pads. This ability to walk on water has labelled the Jacana with the nickname, *Jesus bird.*

That evening, we visit Ubirr and explore the Aboriginal Art sites. Indigenous culture is deep here and some of the rock paintings are estimated to be 4,000 years old. Its atmospheric sitting and soaking up the sunset as we overlook the surrounding wetlands and I feel a deep reverence for the landscape and its years of cultural heritage. As we return to our campsite shortly afterwards, we spot a Short-eared Rock Wallaby amongst the crevices and later a Northern Brushtail Possum, in the trees. Two more exciting first encounters for our wildlife journal.

Comb-Crested Jacana

Early the following morning, we enjoy breakfast at Cahills Crossing and then take a nice wander through the rainforest. Afterwards, we appreciate the shade in the park visitor centre as we watch regional documentaries before continuing onwards to Nourlangie Rock where we have an emotive chat with an Aboriginal guide. We camp at Cooinda that night and listen to Dingo howls atmospherically reverberating across the land, offering a magical end to another wonderful day.

On our final morning in Kakadu, we enjoy an early boat cruise along the Yellow Water River where we see huge amount of Crocodiles in close proximity. An abundance of birdlife is also on display with varieties of Flycatchers, Kingfishers, Geese, Ducks and Terns, providing a glimpse of the enormous diversity of life in the region. We feel truly blessed to have had so many amazing experiences here.

Lily Creek Lagoon, Kununurra. August 2003

On return to Kununurra, we settle back into community life. Work at the Banana Farm has dried up, so I find an alternative in the Melon Fields. It's a hard graft, bent over all day in the hot sun but I have fun with my companions who comprise of: Swedes, Dutch, Irish, British, Australian and New Zealand workers. A truly multinational team!

I love arriving in the early morning light as I regularly see an Australian Bustard, rising its head high as we approach and walking slowly but warily away from us. Sometimes, it breaks into a fast run before taking off into flight with a loud call. It's my first experience with Bustards and those few exhilarating moments are the perfect start to my day.

Australian Bustard

My week day evenings are spent at the gym and playing football games with the locals. At the weekends we attend BBQs and have the odd night out at Gulliver's Tavern. It's a blissful time living within this friendly Kimberley community and we regularly go to the nearby lookout point to enjoy the spectacular sunsets and look fondly at our adopted town.

Our working visas begin to loom ever closer to expiring and I'm sad at the thought of leaving so for a final week treat, my friend Gary brings me for a late evening kayak on Lily Creek Lagoon. We paddle blissfully amongst the mangroves whilst listening to the birdsong chorus and then drift peacefully to enjoy the sunset. As we relax under the glow of the setting sun, a Flying Fox colony takes off from the surrounding trees and begin to skim the water around us. I realise they're belly dipping, as they drink by licking the water from their fur afterwards. It's a mesmerising spectacle to witness and as I soak up the magical scene I feel full with contentment. It's the perfect goodbye and an ideal tribute to celebrate our time in the Kimberley.

Little Red Flying Fox

Recalibration

After our Australian working visa expires, we visit Indonesia. Arriving in Bali initially, we spend a few days at Kuta to settle in and then book on a day trip to Lake Batur which provides an opportunity to appreciate the Balinese countryside. It's fascinating to see how the rice terraces shape much of the landscape and I'm struck by the beauty and contrast they provide.

We enjoy a meal with a stunning view as we overlook Mount Batur, an active volcano which dominates its surrounds. Lingering as long as we can and perhaps inspired by the scenery, we begin to discuss our next travel opportunities.

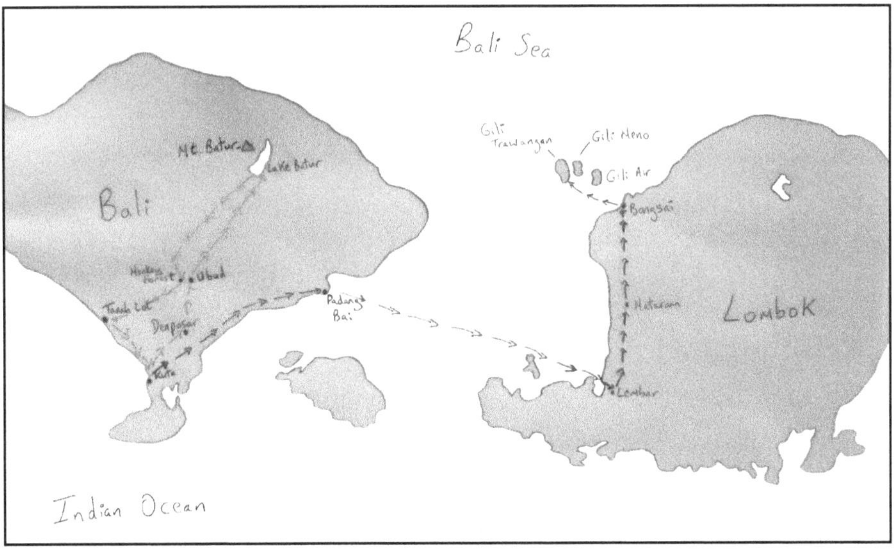

Bali - Lombok - Gili Islands

We've heard about the Gili Islands, off the coast of Lombok and decide they may be the perfect location to offer some recharging time.

Before we leave Bali, we also visit the Monkey Forest at Sangeh and Tanah Lot, an atmospheric and famous Hindu temple which is set on a large rock overlooking the sea. Travelling onwards to Lombok, we then catch a small charter boat to the Gili Islands.

Gill Trawangan, Lombok, Indonesia. September 2003

Arising in our beach side hut in the early morning light, I treat myself to a leisurely swim before breakfast. Feeling refreshed afterwards, I lay contentedly in my hammock and blissfully watch the world pass by. This is a lovely change of pace and provides a perfect opportunity to take stock of our travels and recalibrate.

We spend relaxing days writing, reading, drawing and planning our next steps. Making the most of our exotic location, we also expand our dive experience by completing our Advanced Scuba Certification. Having started dive training a year previously in the Malaysian Perhentian Islands, it feels good to reach this point. Here in the clear tropical waters of the Bali Sea, we spot Cuttlefish, Green Turtles, Giant Clams, Clown Fish, Moray Eels and Stingrays.

We also encounter White Tip Reef Sharks and excitingly, a Faint-banded Sea Snake, swimming fluidly in the open. This is a first time sighting for us and we admire its long striped body. Afterwards, our dive instructor informs us these are amongst the most venomous sea snakes in the world with an extremely toxic potency. Luckily, their mild temperament means they are rarely a threat to humans.

Faint-Banded Sea Snake

Our time on the beautiful island slips by peacefully as we settle into a circadian rhythm, bedding down at sun set and rising naturally at first light. We feel healthy, vibrant and physically in tune. It's the perfect recharging tonic and infuses us with a fresh energy, ready for new adventures.

After our Indonesian break, we return to Australia on a tourist visa to attend Rugby World Cup games. We spend time soaking up the big match atmospheres in Perth, Adelaide and Sydney and witness some incredibly exhilarating contests. It's a vibrant time and whilst in Perth, I avail of the opportunity to visit Mary Hutton, the founder of the 'Free the Bears' fund.

This charitable organisation's mission is to protect, preserve and enrich the lives of bears throughout the world. I arrange to meet at Mary's home based office and am incredibly humbled to spend time in her company. Her forthright determination to eradicate the unnecessary suffering of bears is inspiring and I'm impressed at how she has transformed her life from a regular Perth grandmother into a multi-national animal rights activist. It's heartening to see how this commitment has made such a positive difference and I feel incentivised to help out.

I can't offer much support initially but upon my later return to Ireland, I raise sponsorship funds to rescue a Sloth Bear from the dancing trade in India. These raised finances are used to help finance enrichment sanctuaries for rescued bears and also to fund alternative employment training for their Kalandar Gypsy owners. Through supporting people in this way, Free the Bears, alongside other charities, slowly but surely eradicated the bear dancing trade from the streets of India. It feels good to have played some small part.

Nightcap National Park, New South Wales, Australia. November 2003

Once back in Sydney, we enjoy the familiar sights and sounds of the city for a while before hiring a campervan and driving north. Over the course of a few days, we have fun adventures in Myall Lakes National Park, Port Macquarie and Coffs Harbour before eventually making it to Byron Bay, the most easterly location in mainland Australia. We love our time here and as we reluctantly begin the long return journey to Sydney, we detour to Nightcap National Park.

This stunning location is part of the Gondwana Rainforests of Australia and is listed as a UNESCO World Heritage Area. We take a beautiful walk on the Mount Matheson Loop, spotting Red-legged Pademelons and Australian Brush Turkeys on the way.

Afterwards, I feel energised and decide to continue exploring alone on the Pholis Gap Walk. I'm totally immersed in the invigorating environment and time passes quickly.

As light begins to fade, I hear movement amongst the trackside leaf litter. Assuming it's a Brush Turkey, I freeze and patiently wait for the creature to reveal itself from the undergrowth. Slowly emerging from the vegetation, a rabbit sized animal with dark brown fur and a pointed nose appears, moving its head vigorously from side to side as it sniffs the ground. It excavates the soil, feeding on whatever morsels it finds before ambling back into the shrubby vegetation.

I'm totally intrigued by this special encounter and once back at the parking area, I find information boards which highlight it as a Long-nosed Potoroo, a small marsupial which is part of the Rat Kangaroo family. As a nocturnal creature, it spends the majority of its time in the dense understorey, so I've been incredibly fortunate to view its natural foraging behaviour so clearly.

Long-nosed Potoroo

Later, when we visit Dorrigo National Park, one of the rangers explains how privileged I've been as Potoroos are extremely difficult to spot. As we then explore the trails around Dorrigo, I reflect on the richness of my experience and on the many magical wildlife encounters we've had. Absorbing the lush surrounds of the beautiful rainforest, I listen to the familiar tones of the Eastern Whip Bird and I smile as its whip-crack song resonates around the bush. We've had some incredible adventures, but now it feels like time to go home.

Upon our return, I catch up with family and friends and explore with a new found appreciation and heighted sense for wildlife encounters. This leads to first time sightings of many species and I feel a deeper, more enriching appreciation for Ireland's natural heritage.

This craving for consistent wildlife engagement brings a lot of richness to my life but also means I struggle to settle back into a regular work routine. I acquire a driving job which I generally enjoy but overall I'm restless and eager for more travel adventures. As I continue to work hard, I set an intention for more big travels but I'm also keen to experience and appreciate the beauty of Ireland whilst I can...

Kenmare Bay, County Kerry, Republic of Ireland. August 2005

Sailing out into Kenmare Bay, I admire our stunning location, sandwiched between the Iveragh and Beara Peninsulas. My spirits are high as I admire the splendid views of the distant Cork and Kerry mountains and there's a palpable excitement on board. *Captain Raymond Ross*, regales us with his extensive knowledge of the local area as we cruise along the tranquil waters of the bay.

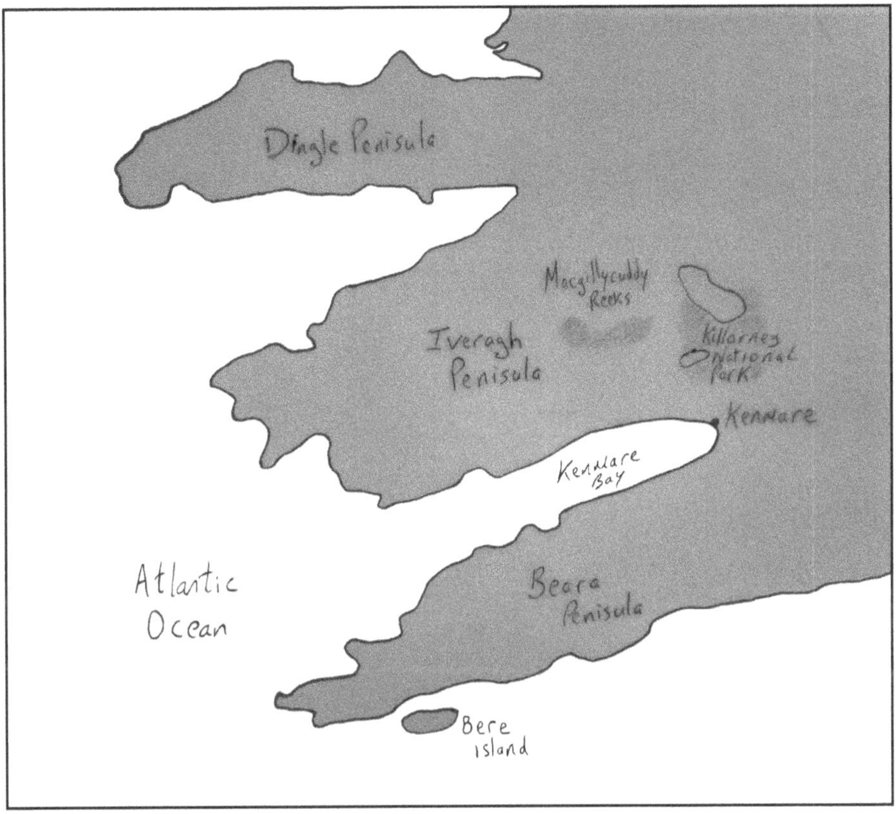

Kenmare Bay

This Eco-nature cruise is bringing us towards one of Ireland's largest Common Seal colonies and as we gradually approach them, we observe their movement on the protruding rock island. Raymond points out the unique hide pattern on each individual and we listen to his tales of Selkies, mythological beings in Celtic and Norse mythology, who change from seal to human form by shedding their skin. It's a captivating and fascinating experience as we bob gently past the colony.

A we continue to explore the bay, we marvel at the sight of Northern Gannets, piercing the water with arrow like ferocity. Renowned for their incredible diving ability, these gregarious seabirds are striking the water at speeds of up to 100kph as they hunt for aquatic prey. Their fast and powerful dives around us offer an exhilarating presence which places them firmly amongst my favourite bird species. As we return to land I feel renewed. My time at home has been incredible and it's reinforced my enthusiasm and passion for wildlife. Now it's time once more for far flung travel adventures.

Northern Gannet

Inspiration

After our time in Ireland, we return to South-east Asia to explore further. Settling in quickly, we reacclimatise in Bangkok before traveling onwards to Chang Mai and then to the spectacular temples at Ayutthaya. It's great to be in Thailand again and we're excited to expand our horizons across this captivating land...

Khao Luk Chang Bat Cave, Khao Yai National Park, Thailand. July 2006

Dusk is falling, we're feeling reinvigorated after a cold and refreshing swim and we're waiting patiently, close to the large cave system of Khao Luk Chang, known affectionately as the *'Bat Cave'*. Between one and three million Wrinkled-lipped Free-tailed Bats are estimated to roost here and we've come to witness their mass emergence.

As the light fades, we notice the first winged mammals emerging and also the birds of prey which have arrived on the scene. Buzzards, Sparrowhawks and Peregrine Falcons, all searching for an opportune moment to pick out an individual, detached from the collective swarm. The Bats start to stream past us, high overhead and staying tight together as the raptors swoop around their fringes.

It's an astounding spectacle as the sky overhead darkens with the swarming masses. The Raptor presence barely impacts the huge collective as they disperse across the landscape and it's easy in this moment to recognise how bats collectively make up almost a quarter of the

Earth's total mammal population. Our guide reminds us they play a vital role in ecosystem health and also help to protect farmland crops by preying on nocturnal insects. His enthusiasm them is infectious.

The following day, we set off on an excursion into the National Park with another experienced guide, affectionately known as '*The Birdman*'. I'm giddy with excitement as we layer up with finely woven anti-leech leggings and can't wait to experience some of the enormous diversity which Khao Yai is so renowned for.

Gerry and Abigail wearing Anti-Leech Socks

After a quick browse at the information centre, Abigail and I, take a walk to Haew Suwat Waterfalls, a scenic location, utilised for the famous jump scene in '*The Beach*' a well watched movie amongst backpackers in South-east Asia. The raw and vibrant energy of the cascading falls is invigorating and we sit captivated on the rocks nearby as we soak up its power.

Downstream, we spot a couple of Chinese Water Dragons, clinging to overhanging tree branches. These impressive reptiles are up to a metre long and are incredibly agile.

They are also powerful swimmers and spend a lot of time close to water courses. If threatened, they can drop into water to swim to safety or remain submerged until the danger has passed. We admire their impressive size and how resplendent they look with their proud alert pose and eye catching banded tail.

Chinese Water Dragon

Once back at the visitor centre, we gather for lunch and then embark on our afternoon excursion with '*The Birdman*'. He lives up to his reputation, finding us an incredible array of wildlife and pointing out animals which we just wouldn't see otherwise. We find Scorpions and Giant Millipedes and then a pair of Lar Gibbons high in the jungle canopy.

A spotting scope enables an intimate glimpse into the world of these endangered primates. The light brown, sandy coloured female nestles her youngster tightly whilst peering suspiciously back at us through the dense foliage. Her male companion lingers close by, looking splendid in his black fur coat. He seems coiled and ready to explode into action. After a few moments of respectful observation, we move quietly away, leaving this arboreal family in peace. It's been a privileged encounter and we embrace the natural

Female Lar Gibbon and Young

Spotting Wildlife

high it has brought to our group. Shortly afterwards, *'The Birdman'* points out a Rhinoceros Hornbill, perched on a prominent branch in the middle distance. Once more, our spotting scope provides an intimate view and we are enthralled by the huge orange and red casque and bill on this impressive bird. I've always had a fascination with Hornbills and the shape and size of their elaborate casque. To me, they are the very epitome of tropical wildlife.

Now, as I focus my attention on the bird in front of me, I admire its magnificent features. *'The Birdman'* explains that Hornbills defend their territories with trumpeting calls and it's believed that their casque acts as a resonating chamber, amplifying their sound across a large distance. This can also help to attract a mate. As we continue onwards across the jungle trails, we soon spot another Hornbill flying overhead. It's thrilling to be in their vicinity and I embrace the warm glow from our magical sightings. It's been such an enriching day, yet as light begins to fade we discover Sun Bear scratchings on a prominent tree trunk. It's a timely reminder that Khao Yai has many more wildlife delights yet to discover.

Rhinocerous Hornbill

After our wildlife adventures at Khao Yai, we travel into Laos, known officially as the Lao People's Democratic Republic (Lao PDR). We enjoy time in the capital, Vientiane before travelling onwards to Vang Vieng where we have a surreal tubing experience down the Nam Song River.

Afterwards we visit the beautiful World Heritage Listed City of Luang Prabang. Staying here for a few days, we soak up the tranquil atmosphere, relaxed travel vibe and delicious food served at nightly outdoor buffets. We sample Buddhist temples and monasteries and travel to the stunning Kuang Si Waterfalls where we also get our first experience of a Free the Bears Sanctuary in South East Asia.

As we journey onwards, we explore Phonsavan and the mysterious Plain of Jars, a bizarre megalithic landscape. Here, thousands of ancient stone jars are scattered across the land, their history and purpose shrouded in mystery. It's atmospheric to wander inquisitively amongst these archaeological ruins.

Stone Jar at The Plain of Jars

Later arriving in Vietnam, we get immersed in the crazy busyness of Hanoi, before embarking on an adventurous expedition to the top of Mount Fansipan, the highest mountain in Indochina at a height of 3,147 metres. We also visit Halong Bay before travelling south to Hoi An and then Nha Trang where we complete our first scuba dives for some time. It feels good to get refresher dives in.

Mountain Guides Assessing the Route on Mount Fansipan

Unfortunately, I have a major relapse of Dengue Fever which I'd first contracted on our travels in 2002. This mosquito-borne tropical disease is sometimes known as 'Breakbone Fever' due to the extreme joint pains it causes. Confined by my aches and burning temperature, we modify our Vietnamese adventures and cut short many plans for wilder explorations.

Luckily after a few days convalescing, I began to feel better and we have a leisurely few days in Ho Chi Minh City, formerly known as Saigon before traveling onwards into Cambodia.

Phnom Tamao Wildlife Rescue Centre, Phnom Penh, Cambodia. 22nd August 2006

Freshly arrived in another country, I feel stronger than I've been for a while and am eager to explore. We hire a motorbike and travel to meet *Matt Hunt*, the newly appointed Chief Executive Officer of *Free the Bears.* We're looking forward to meeting him and getting a feel for the role of the charity in South East Asia.

As we travel through the lush green countryside, I feel the familiar thrill of wanderlust return as I excitedly take stock of our surroundings. Once at Phnom Tamao, we meet *Matt* who provides exclusive behind the scenes access. It's incredible to see the Bears up close and to hear accounts of their harrowing rescues from snares, traps and tiny cages. Alongside extreme habitat loss, Sun Bears are under huge pressure from poachers who trap them for the illegal pet trade or to sell body parts for culinary or medicinal purposes.

Although sanctuary life could never compare to their wild environment, it's uplifting to see the incredible enclosures and enrichment activities provided. *Matt* is clearly a man on a mission and he speaks passionately about his desire to positively change attitudes towards bears and other wildlife in South East Asia. He proudly presents the recently completed wildlife hospital and then offers us the incredible privilege of feeding an orphaned Sun Bear cub.

As I enjoy this magical experience, I feel thankful for the opportunity to meet passionate advocates for the natural world such as *Matt.* Witnessing his fiercely driven determination in front line activism and conservation, I am inspired with hope that humanity hasn't completely lost its way.

Sun Bear

After our South-east Asian adventures we return to Australia to catch up with our family in Perth before journeying onwards to explore Queensland.

Cape Tribulation, Daintree National Park, Queensland, Australia. 2nd October 2006

Standing on the remote headland of Cape Tribulation, I feel full and content as I absorb my surroundings. I'm in a unique location, where two UNESCO World Heritage sites meet; the Wet Tropics Rainforest and the Great Barrier Reef.

Having arrived a couple of days earlier we've already explored trails through the lush green surrounds and enjoyed a cruise on the Daintree River where we spotted numerous large Crocodiles.

Rightfully renowned as one of the most complex ecosystems on earth, the Daintree Rainforest is estimated to be 180 million years old. Within its embrace, it feels as if we've taken a giant step back in time, almost as if dinosaurs could emerge from the undergrowth at any stage. I'm on constant alert for wildlife encounters and I'm particularly keen to spot the large, flightless Cassowary. This prehistoric looking bird is renowned for it's potentially aggressive behaviour and it's a bracing feeling just to know we can happen upon one at any stage. This sense of edginess brings an aliveness to our walks.

In the evening, as I stroll along the beach, a heavy scuttling noise in the undergrowth causes a stir of excitement. Could it be a Cassowary? Emerging from the undergrowth comes a large bird with a crimson red head and a vibrant yellow throat wattle. Not a Cassowary but a male Brush Turkey.

I smile wryly as he scratches the sand sporadically, searching for morsels of food. Although not considered exotic and perhaps even a pest to some, I'm still excited to see him. His presence brings a splash of colour and vibrancy to my day and it's delightful to watch his antics as he moves stealthily between the open sand and surrounding vegetation.

Australian Brush Turkey

As I observe, I reflect upon the thrill which animal encounters bring, especially unexpected ones such as this. Wildlife unpredictability is part of the joy of exploring and this uncertainty has brought a special magic to our adventures.

Later, as we pop out for a nocturnal wander, we find two more enchanting species to add to our sightings list, a Northern Brown Bandicoot and a White-lipped Tree Frog. It's a perfect way to round off our wonderful time in the Daintree National Park.

Travelling south, we then enjoy snippets of time in many beautiful locations such as Mossman Gorge, the Atherton Tablelands and Mission Beach. I miss my opportunity to sight Cassowaries and Tree Kangaroos as we move out of their range but console myself with explorations at Wallaman Falls in Girrigun National Park and on Fraser Island, the largest sand island on the planet.

We also enjoy a contrasting day through visiting the Ginger Factory at Yandina which provides a surreal Willy Wonka type experience. Another incredible highlight is a whale watching tour in Hervey Bay where we enjoy magnificent encounters with Humpback Whales. Overall, our time in Queensland is delightful but is flashing by quickly, so we're keen to fit in one last quick adventure before departure...

Glass House Mountains National Park, Sunshine Coast, Queensland, Australia. 17th October 2006

Sitting out front of our campervan, we enjoy a late evening brew as we overlook the craggy peaks of the Glass House Mountains. We admire the panoramic landscape and reflect on another incredible day which will linger long in our memories.

We've just been to Australia Zoo, home of the iconic Crocodile Hunter, *Steve Irwin*. Our visit is just a few short weeks after his tragic and untimely death yet the zoo team are clearly infused with his spirit and energy. There is undoubted emotion in the air but also a focused determination to carry on his legacy.

The zoo's motto '*Conservation through Exciting Education*' is evident to see as staff embody the message that animals belong in the wild and that we have to preserve land and protect habitat. They speak passionately about endangered species breeding programs, Crocodile research projects and rescuing wildlife in need. It's inspiring and motivating to witness. *Steve's* passion, energy and drive has clearly influenced the team and hardened their conservation resolve.

The love for wildlife at the zoo is contagious and it's positive influence is apparent as it ripples amongst its visitors and out into the wider world. It's been an apt reminder of how our actions and attitudes can activate hope and decisive action and I'm deeply motivated by this wonderful gift. As the sun sets on our amazing Australian adventure, I raise a toast to *Steve* and his inspiring legacy.

Intention

We arrive in New Zealand and settle in quickly, participating in the Auckland Marathon just a few short days after our arrival. After months of backpacking and insufficient training, it's a challenging day but enjoyable nonetheless.

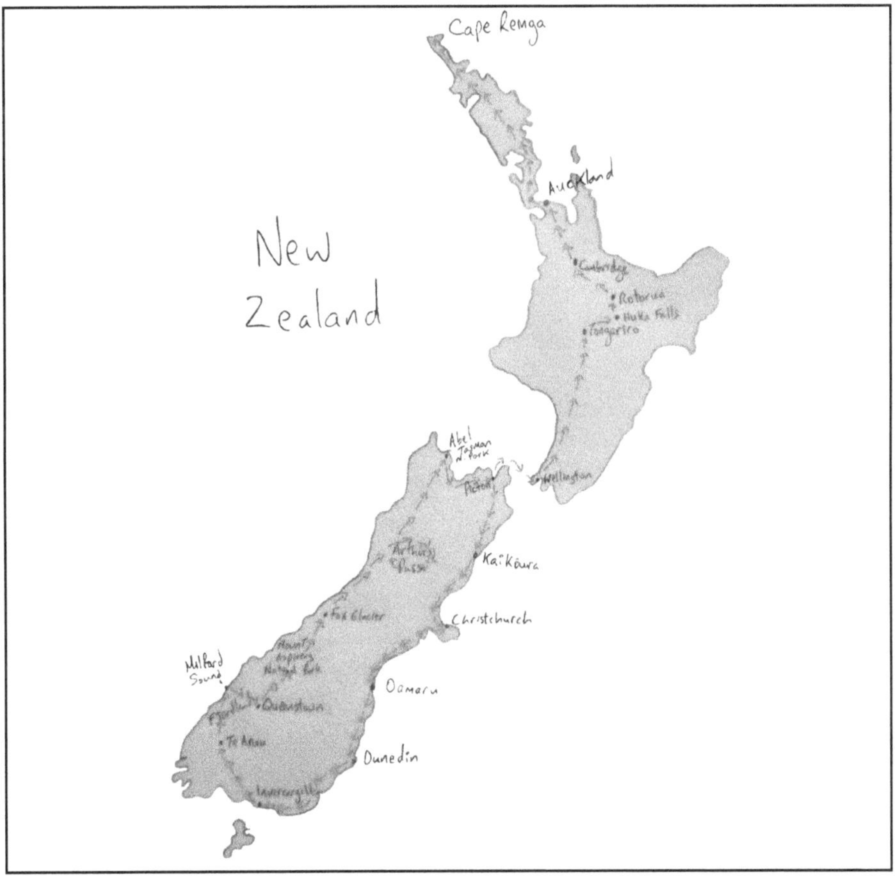

New Zealand

Afterwards we spend a few quiet days of relaxation in the city, during which we take an honest assessment of our finances. Recognising we don't have the budget for an extended stay, we instead decide to hire a campervan and have a whistle-stop tour to experience this diverse land as best we can...

Oamaru, Otago, New Zealand. 9th November 2006

Arriving on the South Island, we travel down the east coast and visit Kaikoura, a small coastal village, renowned for its breath taking views. We sit and admire the stunning location with snow clad mountains looming over a beautiful bay and enjoy the sights and sounds of the native Fur Seal colony.

As we move further down the coast, we have brief

New Zealand Fur Seal

visits to Christchurch and then Dunedin before arriving in Oamaru, known as the Penguin Capital of New Zealand. As well as a Little Penguin colony, Oamaru is also home to the rare and declining Yellow-Eyed Penguin, known as Hoiho in Maori. We visit a beach in late evening with the hope of spotting some and as dusk draws in we're rewarded with the sight of penguins emerging from the water.

They pass within a few metres of us and it's a thrilling experience to be so close to these appealing birds. They are taller and heavier than I expect and look elegant with a pale yellow striped band, extending from the eyes around the back of their head.

A little later, as we participate in a small guided tour, we spot a female and her chick in the coastal shrubbery. Witnessing their momentary vulnerability, I'm struck by the poignancy of the situation. With ever increasing pressures on their population, these birds need all of their natural resilience levels to survive and thrive.

Yellow-Eyed Penguin

Looking upon the mother and chick, a sombre realisation of the true impact of species decline comes over me. Aside from its place in the ecosystem, the Hoiho also has a place in the heritage and culture of the land. If it was to suddenly disappear, we would be another step closer to a degraded, sterile planet.

As we leave the beach, I visualise this Penguin as a representative for all the planet's endangered species, vulnerable yet resistant in the face of human driven pressures. I feel an intention settling in my mentality to step up and start taking positive environmental action. I know the time for this will soon come.

Oamaru - Penguin Capital of New Zealand

The following day we explore Dunedin and take a beautiful drive around the Otago Peninsula. Observing Northern Royal Albatrosses soaring overhead, we marvel at the three metre wingspan and incredible flight endurance of these graceful seabird giants.

It's the wrong time of year for close encounter viewing on land so we content ourselves with watching them soar on the thermals. Some individuals occasionally swoop low and close to us, which highlights their enormous size. It's a marvellous sight.

As we head further south, we pass through the Catlins, a stunning natural landscape with spectacular coastal stretches. Stopping off at Curio Bay, we take a walk along part of the petrified forest, an area with fossils dating back to the Jurassic period.

As we explore, a Yellow-eyed Penguin, unexpectedly appears and heads towards the ocean. It hesitates upon seeing us and we back away to offer space so it'll have the confidence to continue onwards. As it does so, we smile at the distinctive waddling gait which gets it to the water. A little further along we happen unexpectedly upon a Hooker Sealion who growls at us for intruding its space. Its size and well developed mane indicate it is a male and we quickly realise we're between him and the water.

Quickly amending our route to reduce his stress, I feel slightly embarrassed. He's a big boy and we definitely don't want to get on the wrong side of him. Enthusiasm for wildlife spotting is one thing but it's important to do so with minimum disturbance to the animal.

Milford Sound, Fiordland National Park, New Zealand. 14th November 2006

It's hard to believe possible, but the scenery just keeps getting better. We're continually surrounded by mountains, lakes, forests and waterfalls. Staying at the lovely town of Te Anau for a night, we have our first encounters with the Kea, a large Parrot with olive green plumage. Known affectionately as the '*clown of the mountains*' due to their curious nature, these characters are not shy about getting up close and personal.

As we stop to admire a panoramic landscape, a small flock descend on our van and began to wreak havoc. They pull at the windscreen wipers and rubber sealing on the rooftop and look at us disdainfully as we try to shoo them off.

We realise when we chat with other tourists that Kea investigation is a common theme. It's cute initially but also a bit worrying especially with a hired vehicle. In the end, it's a relief to drive through the Homer Tunnel, a long passageway through the mountains, to escape their insatiable curiosity.

Kea

Emerging on the other side, the road winds down through a picturesque valley to the shore of Milford Sound. After a tranquil lunch on the water front, we take an afternoon cruise on the sound and revel in the raw natural splendour around us. It's perhaps the most stunningly beautiful landscape I've found myself in and I absorb every moment of time here.

We briefly spot Fiordland Crested Penguins, with their funky yellow eyebrow stripes standing out dramatically but as we come closer, they disappear in the choppy waters.

New Zealand Fur Seals are also encountered before an unexpected sighting of a Leopard Seal basking on the shore. This huge individual even looks intimidating from our middle distance range and the Captain highlights our luck at finding him as they're mainly found inhabiting the Antarctic pack ice.

Leopard Seal

Sightings in New Zealand are not rare but definitely not common place and his presence adds a bonus to what is already an exhilarating day. As we return to land, we're full of youthful vigour and as we camp at Cascade Creek that night, we vow that a return visit to Fiordland is a must someday.

The rest of our South Island New Zealand adventure slips by quickly as we experience Queenstown and then the Fox and Franz Josef Glaciers before moving on to Mount Aspiring National Park and then Arthur's Pass. We also spend a day at Abel Tasman National Park and explore the beautiful coastal track. It's all a bit rushed but we're just thankful for having the opportunity to visit these incredible locations.

Once back on the North Island, we return to Auckland to attend the *U2 Vertigo Tour* and have an incredibly atmospheric night, which keeps us on a high for days afterwards. We also squeeze in time to visit the Bay of Islands and travel to Cape Reinga, New Zealand's northernmost point.

A trip to Rotorua enables us to witness its famous geysers and hot mud pools and we also hike through the dramatic volcanic landscape of Tongariro.

Later, camping by spectacular Huka Falls along the Waikato River, we are blown away by its phenomenal raw power and vibrancy. We also visit many *Lord of the Rings* locations, most notably Matamata, home of *Hobbiton* which is an exciting day out.

Overall, we have an exhilarating time making ever-lasting memories in this stunning land of contrast. Our only regret is we don't have longer to explore. Nevertheless, I'm thankful for my experiences and as I reflect on them, I know they have intensified my desire to work proactively for wildlife and the environment.

Tongariro National Park

A couple of days before we depart New Zealand, I sit under a huge tree in the quaint town of Cambridge and set an objective to work within conservation. As I release this intention, I trust the opportune moments will present themselves to me when the time is right.

Action

Upon return from our travels, we settle into life at the heart of the National Forest, an inspiring area in the English Midlands. This visionary multi-purpose forest is being created across 200 square miles of industrially scarred landscape and it's an exciting place to find ourselves. With miles of trails around newly formed country parks and developing woodlands, I explore with an eager zealousness.

Within a couple of months, I have a lucky breakthrough and gain employment as an Environmental Education Ranger at a busy visitor centre. Here, I begin to develop valuable experience in outdoor leadership and wildlife surveying. I also establish skills in woodland and wetland management and begin to network with proactive environmental organisations such as Butterfly Conservation (BC) and The Conservation Volunteers (TCV).

It's a steep learning curve and I embrace it fully, throwing myself into all aspects of the job role. With time, this leads to a Head Ranger promotion which provides a perfect opportunity to deepen relations with conservation groups. I do this through developing symbiotic partnerships, which provide training opportunities for conservation students whilst also providing space for wildlife monitoring and habitat enrichment projects.

Conkers Discovery Centre, Moira, Leicestershire, UK. July 2009

In the late evening light as we finish setting up the generators, I spot two small hunched shapes in the middle distance. As we approach, they run away with a loping gait, bringing to mind Brown Hares, but when they stop in a clearing, I realise they are Muntjac Deer. Originally from China and introduced into the UK at the start of the 20th Century, this species is now widespread across southern and central England.

I regularly hear their loud and piercing bark resonating across the woodland and it's always exciting to happen upon them unexpectedly. I smile as they disappear into the trees and acknowledge the sighting as a positive omen... we're in for a good night of wildlife engagement.

Once fully set up, we warm up with hot drinks and patiently wait. Around us the darkness begins to intensify and we focus inwards on the illuminated white sheets. The first insect arrivals start to appear, intermittently at first but then more rapidly and consistently. Macro and micro Moths are landing with intent, drawn by the irrepressible glow we've created.

My night time colleagues, members of the East Midlands Butterfly Conservation Group, begin to record the diversity and number of species which appear as they contrast perfectly against the bright background. I'm impressed by their knowledge and skill as they identify tiny micro moths with seemingly a brief glance. Years of *'in the field'* monitoring have enabled this level of confidence and I'm full of admirable respect.

Moth trapping and recording such as this is essential work as it develops a greater awareness of species distribution and their population trends. Necessary management plans can then be implemented where possible to prevent declines and to promote recovery.

As the night progresses, I'm mostly drawn to the Hawkmoths, which are the largest and easiest to recognise. Poplar Hawkmoths seem huge as they land, their relatively large and tattered looking wingspan providing an unusual profile and Elephant Hawkmoths also appear in abundance with their unmistakable pink and green colouration.

I'm enthralled by the vibrant presence they provide. Eyed Hawkmoths initially seem plain in comparison, but then show us their hidden complexity by flashing the large blue eyespots on their hind wings. This impressive display is an amazing evolutionary strategy and is used as a form of mimicry to deter predators.

As a variety of Moths continue to appear, I struggle to keep up with all the names and interesting facts my learned colleagues are offering. It's a truly eye opening experience and I'm conscious that I was mainly oblivious to their wonderful diversity beforehand. As I begin to process this, a Privet Hawkmoth appears with its chocolate brown wings and pink and black striped abdomen. It's a beautiful specimen, fittingly adding an extra sprinkling of magic to the occasion.

Privet Hawk Moth ©Steve Plant (2009)

Afterwards as I return to normal routine, I carry a different mindset, regularly scanning nooks and crannies for insects and monitoring those which have been attracted by outside lights. It's a whole new world and brings an exciting new dimension to my wildlife experiences.

I continue my good relations with Butterfly Conservation and begin working alongside *Ken Orpe*, a passionate conservationist and committed invertebrate recorder. Together, we establish new butterfly monitoring sites in South Derbyshire, where weekly transects are carried out to establish the health of local populations.

This is vital work, especially during times of climate change. As indicator species, invertebrate populations paint a picture of the health of the wider environment and serious declines can offer a strong indication that an ecosystem is in decline. Records from transects are submitted to the UK Butterfly Monitoring Scheme which is one of the world's longest running insect monitoring programs and an important resource for analysing change.

Alongside *Ken* and fellow enthusiasts, we establish as much data as possible and are delighted when we record Dingy Skipper in some new locations. This species has become increasingly rare across Britain and Ireland and is listed nationally as a high conservation priority.

With *Ken*'s guidance, we establish volunteer work parties to enhance their habitat and to boost opportunities for the species to thrive locally. I take great pride in this work and it feels incredibly meaningful to have involvement in proactive conservation. It offers hope that all is not lost and highlights the immense value of working collaboratively for wildlife.

Dingy Skipper ©Derek Brownlee (2009)

Big Moor, Peak District National Park, UK. October 2011

It's been a long time since I've been to the Peaks and my friends *Ian Kenny* and *Tony Smith* have encouraged me to come and explore for the day. It's just the tonic needed, after a difficult personal period which led to me stepping away from the ranger job role I loved so much. As soon as I take in the fresh moorland air, I wonder why I've not come to the Eastern Edges sooner. It's a stunning location and a perfect place to reset and attune to the Earth's natural rhythms.

I feel revitalised as I enjoy the good company of friends and I rapidly sense my adventurous streak returning. As I scramble up around Burbage Edge I'm enthralled to see bullet holes in the boulders and find out they were used as target practise for soldiers during World War 2. I visualise how life must have been here at that time and as I embrace the peaceful surrounds, I offer my gratitude for today's serenity.

Once up on Big Moor, we hear the bellow of a Red Deer stag resonating across the landscape. It's the early stages of rutting season and the big males are beginning to assert dominance with their primeval call.

As the bellow reverberates across the moor, it evokes a sense of wildness and we feel as if we've stepped back in time. Moving steadily around the moorland edge we eventually spot the stag and some hinds in the distance. Staying downwind, we crouch low to break our outline against the sky and then as we get closer, we begin to crawl through the heather.

Stopping at a respectful distance, *Ian* manages to capture incredible photographs of the Deer in the late afternoon light. I'm content observing their interactions and I admire the strength and command of the majestic male. Something about his essence, reignites my spark. I feel my resolve hardening and a passion burning within to continue working hard for wildlife. I sense an impulse to step up again, to take back control and embody my leadership qualities.

As we leave the moors later that day, the intention to continue my conservation journey has already settled deep within my psyche.

Red Deer ©Ian Kenny (2011)

Shortly afterwards, I begin to submit monthly wildlife articles to the local newspaper and get back out in the community, delivering ranger presentations and wildlife talks. I start an Honours degree in Environmental Studies with the Open University and sign up as a volunteer ranger within the Peak District National Park.

Here, I receive extensive training in navigation, mountain safety, first aid, and wildlife and countryside matters. Throughout this training phase, I visit various briefing centres, gaining experience on ranger patrols across a variety of landscapes.

Once fully qualified, I'm assigned to a rota position in the Goyt Valley where I develop a deep appreciation for the history and wildness of the region. Patrolling the moors, I regularly experience the rattling call of Red Grouse as I watch them erupting rapidly from the heather. I also spot large flocks of Golden Plover and on a few special occasions I witness the incredible rolling, tumbling display flights of Lapwing as they move with incredible speed through the sky.

On late summer evenings, I sit atop Shining Tor as the sun sets and listen to the evocative call of the curlew as it echoes across the land. This time is precious and I feel rich and content from my experiences.

Peak District Navigation

In addition to ranger patrols in the Goyt Valley, I explore the wider Peak District and have many wonderful adventures. Days with Ian on the Kinder Plateau are especially memorable as we search for Mountain Hares in their white winter coats. The rugged landscape and changing seasons bring constant delight and it seems as if there is enough incentive to contain me here for quite a while. However, a serendipitous opportunity for a full time Ranger position pops up in an entirely different region which offers new and exciting wildlife opportunities...

Forest of Dean, Gloucestershire, UK. September 2015

Moving through the forest in the dark, I hear the heavy movement of large animals ahead. Pausing, I signal to my group to remain quiet, keep their torch lights low and to follow my lead. We move slowly out into the clearing and stand quietly for a few moments in the dark.

Ahead, we hear the snuffling, grunting and occasional squeals of feral Wild Boar. Now we're settled, I focus my infra-red spotlight onto the animals ahead. We see large females, juvenile males and the striped piglets known affectionately as *'Humbugs'*. They're all rooting on the forest floor, using their long snout and powerful neck muscles to rotavate the soil in search of anything edible; roots, tubers, bulbs, worms, beetles, bugs, grubs and fallen nuts and berries.

The boar are consumed with the process and seem oblivious to our presence. Due to their short sightedness, standing quietly from a safe distance is the best way to observe this natural behaviour. Whilst for me this is a regular occurrence, I delight at the experience and love providing opportunities for others to enjoy this ancient natural spectacle.

Although the Wild Boar presence in the Forest of Dean can be an emotive subject, there is no doubt they promote a sense of wildness and an impression of awe and wonder amongst those who crave natural connections.

As well as Boar, my nocturnal adventures lead to regular encounters with Foxes, Bats and Tawny Owls as well as

Wild Boar in Camera Trap

Fallow, Roe and Muntjac Deer. Sometimes I happen upon totally unexpected species such as Badgers and Polecats. On one memorable night, an Otter appeared in front of me. On another occasion, a hazel Dormouse ran across a clearing and obligingly moved up along the grass stalks to provide a stunning view. As an animal which spends the majority of its life tucked up in its nest or climbing secretly amongst tree branches, this was an incredibly fortuitous sighting.

Project Pine Marten

As my ranger career progresses, an exciting opportunity becomes available to have involvement in a feasibility study to return a long lost woodland resident, the Pine Marten.

Driven to local extinction in Victorian times, Scotland had become the last British stronghold for this mustelid until a successful reintroduction to mid-Wales in 2015. Alongside, the re-established Welsh population, it is now hoped that a follow up reintroduction in the Forest of Dean and Lower Wye Valley will provide the necessary genetic diversity to safeguard the species in lowland Britain.

Over two years, as a core volunteer, I become heavily involved in Squirrel damage surveys, habitat assessments and camera trap monitoring as well as public engagement and fund raising to support the initiative. Finally in September 2019, alongside other volunteers and staff from Gloucestershire Wildlife Trust and Forestry England we celebrate as Pine Martens are officially returned to the woodland home where they had previously dwelt.

The return of this mid-range predator to the forest offers ongoing support in restoring natural balance and

Radio Tracking Pine Marten ©Josie Bridges (2015)

driving ecological processes. In all the gloom of global species decline, it's heartening to have had involvement in this proactive environmental initiative and to work alongside committed and dedicated conservationists to create meaningful change.

Pine Marten

Hope

As I continue my immersive ranger work, I lead regular interactive activities in the forest and engage consistently with local schools and community groups. My woodland 'office' is an enjoyable place to be and over time I develop a deep sense of its natural rhythms. My days are gratifying and I'm content and happy but as ever, my adventurous mindset is always seeking opportunities for new wildlife encounters...

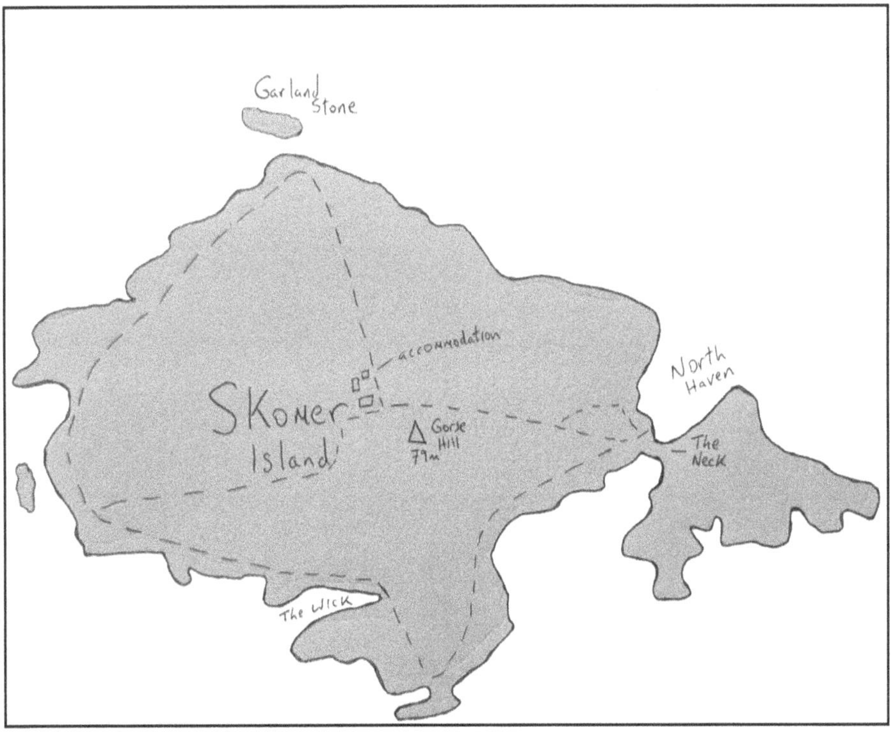

Skomer Island

Skomer Island, Pembrokeshire, Wales, UK. September 2018

An impact thud on the window startles our group. It's starting to darken and the warden informs us the Shearwaters are beginning to arrive. He ends his briefing abruptly, switches lights off to reduce further collisions and shepherds us outside with our red filtered torches so we can monitor the influx.

Approximately half of the world's breeding population of Manx Shearwater are found on the Welsh Islands of Skomer and Skokholm and we're here as Wildlife Trust volunteers to help gauge their health and abundance. This medium sized seabird, renowned for its phenomenal flight capacity, travels on long distance migrations to South America every winter and returns for the summer months. One purposeful individual, ringed on Bardsey Island in 1957, has been calculated to have flown over 5 million miles in its lifetime.

However graceful they are in flight, Shearwaters are extremely clumsy on land and as we wander through their massive colony we witness many individuals crash landing into the undergrowth before moving with an awkward shuffling gait towards their burrows. They've spent the day at sea and are returning to feed their hungry chicks.

Their raucous cackling calls echo around the island and its incredibly evocative as we stand in their midst. I am overwhelmed by the sheer intensity of the experience as the remote black darkness of the island and the cacophony of bird noise combine to create a mesmerising atmosphere.

Manx Shearwater

The following morning, I explore the island trails and spot Grey Seal pups, Greater and Lesser Black Backed Gulls, Ravens, Kittiwakes, Choughs, Fulmars, Guillemots, Razorbills and Short-eared Owls. Having already been on Skomer in early summer to see the Puffins, I know the trails well and am happy to leisurely explore and enjoy the coastal scenery.

By afternoon, along with other volunteers, we're back with the wardens to monitor the Shearwater chick population. Under supervision, we reach into designated burrows and extract fluffy youngsters to be weighed and health checked.

It's vital data which contributes to the long term monitoring of the population and I feel extremely privileged to be involved. The experience of holding these chicks whilst visualising the endurance flights they'll be soon undertaking is very humbling.

Manx Shearwater Chick

As I delicately return them to their burrows I find it hard to believe they'll be robust enough but I am assured by the wardens that they are healthy and perfectly on course. These birds are truly a remarkable species. That night, we once more witness the enlivening sights and sounds of adult birds returning in huge numbers. It's hard to get enough of the mesmerising spectacle and we linger long into the night to soak it up as much as we can.

Once the birds gradually quieten and settle, we relax and admire the night sky with the benefit of zero light pollution. Perhaps inspired, one of our group suggests we complete an island Toad count and within moments we are all busy once more across the trails, collectively recording the abundant amphibians.

In total, we add over 500 Common Toads to the island's wildlife log before we eventually retire contently to our accommodation. It's been a long and eventful day, rich and full with adventure.

Forest of Dean, Gloucestershire, UK. – Summer 2019

Back in the forest, I involve myself with extensive volunteer work relating to bats. Alongside fellow enthusiasts, I complete hedgerow surveys across the Lower Wye Valley and Forest of Dean. These assessments are undertaken close to Greater and Lesser Horseshoe roost sites, so that flight path connectivity can be enhanced.

Although not exclusively dependent on this flight behaviour, Horseshoe Bats are renowned for following linear features such as woodland edges and hedgerows. It is thought that perhaps this may aid their navigation and offer protection from predation and wind.

As such, we map and record notable hedgerow gaps so they can be connected. I find myself continuously thinking like a Bat, assessing regularly if I would fly across a noticeable hedgerow gap if in the animals position. My hours surveying are fitted in on top of my regular ranger position and the days sometimes are long and tiring. However, it feels meaningful and rewarding and my commitment pays off as I'm offered a position on an exciting conservation project.

Standing by a hedgerow in the breaking dawn light, I wear a tired smile as I listen to intermittent warbles. Set at 82khz, my heterodyne bat detector is picking up the echolocation calls of Greater Horseshoe Bats as they return to their roost after a night time of foraging. They're travelling surprisingly fast as they follow the hedge line in front of me and without a detector, I'd struggle to notice them whizzing by.

It's the final stages of a prolonged period of radio-tracking study, carried out under licence by Natural England. Our small dedicated team have been tracking female bats throughout the summer, to assess if there is a variance in flight and foraging behaviours, pre and post maternity.

Greater Horseshoe Bat ©David Priddis (2019)

Horseshoe Bats emit high ultrasonic calls through their nose unlike other British Bats which do so through their mouth. The horseshoe-shaped nose-leaf, from which they derive their name, concentrates these calls into a narrow beam of sound which helps them to navigate and hunt.

It's a labour intensive process and long dark hours are spent covering miles of forest tracks to pick up the signals of tagged females. It's tiring yet exhilarating work. Sometimes, hours pass with little success, but once a female is located, our adrenaline surges and team members swoop into action to gain accurate triangulation fixes.

The data is compiled to map out flight-ways and develop greater understanding of feeding behaviours, thus ensuring necessary knowledge is in place to safeguard against disturbance. The information also creates an understanding of where flight path enhancements can be made. It is critically important data to aid the conservation of a protected species.

Greater Horseshoe Bats Before Release

Our long nightly tracking escapades provide plenty of opportunities for wildlife encounters and we regularly spot Fallow, Roe and Muntjac Deer as well as occasional Badgers, Foxes, Hedgehogs, Wild Boar and Tawny Owls. On two successive mornings, I'm also lucky enough to see a Barn Owl quartering across a rough grassland meadow.

However, the stars of the show are without doubt the Greater Horseshoe Bats. As it's my first time working closely with the species, I find it an enjoyable learning curve. I feel very privileged collaborating with experts who offer huge commitment towards the conservation of this rare mammal.

As with many other species, the Greater Horseshoe's distribution range and population has declined dramatically so it's extremely uplifting to experience first-hand the dedicated work offered towards their protection.

As the weeks progress, I feel my understanding of Bat ecology developing enormously and one night towards the end of the survey period, I witness first-hand how hedgerow gaps can impact flight patterns.

As I intently track a female departing the roost, she flies directly along the hedge-line towards the road, where I stand. Just before she reaches the clearing she abruptly turns 180 degrees and heads back the way she has come. It's fascinating to witness and reinforces the importance of enhancing flight line connectivity in core Horseshoe sustenance zones.

Greater Horseshoe Bat

Forest of Dean, Gloucestershire, UK. January 2020

Squeezing through an almost impossibly tight space, I abruptly emerge into a vast open cavern. As I take in our surrounds, I notice multiple side chambers vanishing into the dark. Our small team busily activates into action and we work in organised coordination to ensure every nook, cranny and cavity is explored. We're searching for hibernating Bats and compiling an extensive list of the species and numbers recorded.

Contrary to popular belief, most of the Bats are not hanging high overhead but sometimes on clefts just a few inches off ground level or in tiny cavities in the rock face. Extreme concentration is required for every hand and foot placement and its imperative to operate under strict guidelines to ensure no disturbance or injury occurs.

These Bat sites of the Forest of Dean and Lower Wye Valley are designated as a Special Area of Conservation (SAC) due to their high concentrations of Horseshoe Bats. The annual winter surveys through the disused mines and caves offer an indication as to how well their populations are doing.

On this day, we record vast numbers of Lesser horseshoe but also Bechstein's, Brown Long-eared, Daubenton's, Greater Horseshoe, Natterer's and Whiskered Bats. By the end of the day, we're filthy with clay, mud and iron ore extract and our muscles and limbs ache from hours of crawling and moving with concentrated focus.

Nonetheless, every member of our team is smiling broadly from our glimpse into this secretive world and we feel ecstatic to have recorded so many diverse and fascinating animals.

Upon return to my car, I reflect on my journey over the last few years. My experiences with wildlife have intensified and it's been an incredible privilege to be involved directly with species conservation through research and monitoring projects.

I've witnessed the hard work, commitment and sacrifice many individuals offer to protect wildlife against the odds of global biodiversity decline. It presents hope for the future and an indication that all is not lost.

As I drive home, I reflect to my childhood and the image of the Proboscis Monkey which so captivated me. The fascination he inspired, encouraged a quest for wildlife adventures which have enriched my life profoundly.

It's been quite a journey and I recognise I still have the same sense of awe as I think about the hibernating Bats hanging from their rock clefts. I muse about future possibilities and realise: I have no idea what's next on my life path.

One thing I'm certain of though, is if I continue to follow the *'Wildlife Whispers'* which encourage me onwards, I'll live a rich and rewarding life, crammed full of magic and wonder.

Preparing to Write

Afterword

Working on this book has brought the memory of some amazing animal encounters vividly back to life. There are many more experiences which haven't make the final cut but all are equally valid. Even those times when I missed out on wildlife which I was desperate to see have been enriching and magical. Noticeable examples of near misses include: Pygmy Elephants, Tree Kangaroos and Cassowaries. Although obviously disappointed to not sight those amazing species, I found just being in their habitat exhilarating enough.

Reflecting on my adventures, I realise how influential my formative years growing up in the Irish countryside were. The freedom and encouragement I had, to enjoy and explore outdoors, forged a deep and meaningful connection with the natural world.

This has remained throughout my life and when times have been challenging, the soothing embrace of nature has held and supported me. On some level this is true for all of us. The simple pleasures of sitting by a tree, feeling the grass on your feet, listening to birdsong or watching the clouds rolling by are all excellent ways to reduce anxiety and stress levels.

A few minutes embracing any of these simple activities can help us to feel calm and potentially make an enormous difference to our well-being. Spending more time in nature also leads to more encounters with many of the wonderful creatures we share this planet with, which will invite surprise, delight and joy into your life.

I wish you well on your own personal wildlife adventures. Enjoy the magic.

Get Involved

There are multiple conservation organisations that are making a positive difference. Through membership support, you can boost your awareness of wildlife and environmental issues whilst also backing their cause. You may even be able to deepen your involvement and develop hands on skills and experiences through volunteering.

Research what options are available to you. It's important to follow your passion, if you love Butterflies, join Butterfly Conservation and become active within your county branch. Get involved with practical conservation work such as habitat management and carry out Butterfly surveys and transects. Or deviate towards Moth recording or administration or fund raising roles. There's a variety of opportunities available to suit whatever your particular desire or skill set may be.

Likewise if Bats appeal, you can become a member of the Bat Conservation Trust and also join your local county branch where you'll get a feel for opportunities close to you. You may be able to assist at Roost Emergence Counts or Bat Box Surveying and even eventually train towards a Bat Licence should you want to develop in this direction.

Or you can get involved in Bat rehabilitation, working alongside specialist carers to get injured and grounded Bats back to full health. The possibilities are broad once you dip your toe into wildlife conservation and you'll find yourself drawn into an immersive world, which provides enriching experiences.

Below, are some ideas to pique your interest which highlight the variety of ways you can get involved in conservation projects. It is best to contact the organisations directly for full details. Although these are predominantly UK based, there may be similar opportunities in other countries.

There are many benefits to getting involved: making new friends, quality time outdoors, learning and developing new skills, possible up close encounters with wildlife and a feel good factor in the knowledge that you're making a positive difference.

Bat Conservation Trust

Become a member. Attend training events, offer support through donations or fundraising or get involved with your local group. They offer opportunities to become involved in surveys or in Bat rescues through working alongside registered carers.

https://www.bats.org.uk

Bumblebee Conservation Trust

Become a member, develop your identification skills and perhaps take part in a '*Bee Walk*' to help develop understanding of Bumblebee populations.

https://www.bumblebeeconservation.org

Butterfly Conservation

Become a member. Get involved with your regional group. Take part in the Big Butterfly Count and record the species that visit your garden.

https://butterfly-conservation.org

Free the Bears

Become a member. Raise funds for rescued Bears. Increase your awareness of the pressures they face. Spread the word. Become active with your country branch. Volunteer at a sanctuary.

https://freethebears.org

Froglife

Become a member. Enhance your garden for amphibians. Take part in local Toad patrols.

https://www.froglife.org

British Hedgehog Preservation Society

Become a member. Make your garden or allotment hedgehog friendly. Avoid the use of pesticides. Make a compost heap. Provide gaps in your fence for animals to move between gardens. Provide supplementary hedgehog friendly meals such as meat-based cat or dog food. If you find an individual which looks sick, injured or underweight, put it in a box in a quiet indoors space whilst you contact your local Hedgehog carer or the British Hedgehog Preservation Society. Work with your neighbours to make your community as Hedgehog friendly as possible.

https://www.britishhedgehogs.org.uk

Royal Society for the Protection of Birds (RSPB)

Become a member. Visit the reserves. Develop your bird knowledge. Take part in the Big Garden Bird Watch. Research conservation volunteering opportunities.

https://www.rspb.org.uk

Wildfowl and Wetland Trust (WWT)

Become a member. Visit the reserves. Learn more about the proactive conservation work which the organisation is carrying out. Talk to staff about involvement possibilities.

https://www.wwt.org.uk

Wildlife Trust

Become a member of your local county branch. Get a feel for the wildlife on your patch. See what opportunities are available to you for active volunteering.

https://www.wildlifetrusts.org

Get Started on Your Own

Rewild an available patch of land

If you have a garden space, perhaps it is possible to rewild totally, or at least to leave a wild corner. It's pretty easy to do - just keep it natural by stopping any pesticide use, letting the grass grow long, embracing the 'weeds' and allowing nature to thrive. It may feel difficult initially but through stepping back and letting go, insect numbers to your patch should increase dramatically. As the nucleus of most food chains, they in turn may attract mammals, birds and reptiles.

If possible you could install a water feature such as a pond, create dead wood piles and plant native perennials which will provide shelter and sustenance for many creatures. Even if you don't have access to a garden, you may be able to provide a window box full of herbs, plants or flowers. There are many ways to support wildlife at this local level and endless book and internet resources are on hand to offer ideas and inspiration.

One of my favourites books on the subject is: *Rewild Your Garden: Create a Haven for Birds, Bees and Butterflies by* Frances Tophill.

A useful internet site is: *Rewild Your Garden: 10 Easy Things You Can Do To Make A Big Difference.*

https://www.ruralsprout.com/rewild-your-garden

Final Note

Even without any 'hands on' involvement we can help, just by enjoying and appreciating all the wonderful interactions we have with the natural world. Through enthusing about wildlife and chatting passionately about nature, we are acknowledging and appreciating the beauty it brings to our lives. We may even recognise that its true value is far beyond any monetary amount. With this wonder so instilled, it's a guarantee that we'll always fight to protect and preserve our wonderful natural heritage.

Star Species

The International Union for Conservation of Nature (IUCN) offers a Red List which provides a comprehensive source of information on the global extinction risk status of animals, plants and fungus species.

All of the following information supplied on; conservation status, range, population trends and threats have been taken from the IUCN Red List website (www.iucnredlist.org) and the Butterfly Conservation website (https://butterfly-conservation.org).

These are incredible resources and I encourage you to explore them to see how your favourite animals are affected, if they are thriving or declining and how you can further support them.

Australian Brush Turkey (Alectura Lathami)

Male Brush Turkeys build large mounds of organic matter for females to lay their eggs. A single mound can be as large as one metre wide by four metres high and several females may deposit their eggs here. Sometimes there may be as many as 50 eggs in a clutch. The eggs are incubated by the heat of the rotten vegetation and a male Brush Turkey will maintain a constant temperature check by inserting his beak in the mound to assess the heat. If needed he'll then add or remove organic matter to achieve the desired temperature. Many eggs are lost to burrowing predators such as Goannas. Once chicks hatch they are fully feathered and independent straight away. They can fly within a few hours of hatching.

Geographic Range: Resident to Australia, ranging from Cape York in far North Queensland to the Sydney suburbs and the Illawara Region of New South Wales.

Conservation Status: Least Concern.

Population Trend: Decreasing.

Threats: Habitat destruction including disappearance and fragmentation of rainforests.

Australian Bustard (Ardeotis Australis)

One of Australia's largest birds, the Bustard has a distinctive walk as it struts along with its neck and head held high. When disturbed, they initially walk away slowly whilst intently watching before breaking into a fast run if they feel in danger. They sometimes break into a strong flight if necessary. Newly hatched chicks have dark and light stripes and remain camouflaged in cover to avoid been seen. Bustards are omnivores and eat a variety of food ranging from fruits, seeds and buds to frogs, lizards and invertebrates. They can communicate through a distinctive high pitched whistle and also have a loud 'carr-ack' call in flight.

Geographic range: Occurs across Continental Australia and occasionally in Southern Papua New Guinea and Papua (Indonesia).

Conservation Status: Least Concern.

Population Trend: Decreasing.

Threats: Livestock farming and ranching, Human intrusions, Invasive species, Hunting and trapping, Agricultural and Forestry Pollution.

Australian Sea Lion (Neophoca Cinerama)

Males (bulls) can weigh up to approximately 300kgs, females (cows) up to 105kg. Australian Sea Lions are polygynous, meaning that one male can mate with multiple females. Bulls engage in fights to ascertain mating rights. They have excellent climbing ability and can sometimes be seen up to 30 metres high on cliffs. Young Sea Lions are called pups and they regularly swim in rock pools to develop their hunting skills in a safe and secure environment. When diving, Sea Lions close their nostrils, only opening them again when they come up for air. They have an incredibly efficient swimming technique, by using their front flippers in a wing like motion and their rear flippers as rudders.

Geographic Range: Endemic to Australia (South Australia and Western Australia).

Conservation Status: Endangered.

Population Trend: Decreasing.

Threats: Residential and commercial development, Agriculture and aquaculture, Disruption from shipping corridors, Human intrusions and disturbance, Overfishing and Climate change and severe weather.

Bornean Orangutan (Pongo Pygmaeus)

Orangutans are arboreal, spending their vast majority of time in the canopy. They are the heaviest tree-dwelling animal, utilising vast areas of forest to forage and mate. They create sleeping nests each night by pulling several large branches together. Orangutans have a huge arm span and can reach their ankles when standing upright. Young Orangutans stay with their mother until they are about seven years old.

Geographic Range: Endemic to the island of Borneo, occurring in the Malaysian states of Sarawak and Sabah as well as Indonesia (Kalimantan).

Conservation Status: Critically Endangered.

Population Trend: Decreasing.

Threats: Habitat Fragmentation, Logging and timber harvesting, Agriculture and Aquaculture, Hunting and trapping, Population. Fragmentation and Continuing decline of mature individuals.

Comb-crested Jacana (Irediparra Gallinacea)

It's habit of walking across floating vegetation gives the impression that it is walking on water which explains its nickname, the Jesus Bird. They bob their head and flick their tail continuously as they search for food such as aquatic insects on the water surface. One female may mate with several males. The male builds the nest, incubates the eggs and cares for the young. If danger threatens the young, he will pick the chicks up, tuck them under his wings and carry them off to safety.

Geographic Range: Australia, Indonesia, Malaysia, Papua New Guinea, The Philippines, Timor-Leste.

Conservation Status: Least Concern.

Population Trend: Unknown.

Threats: Loss of wetland habitat.

Common Wombat (Vombatus Ursinus)

Unlike other marsupials, Wombats have a backward facing pouch which enables them to dig extensively without getting dirt inside it. Their toughened backside is mostly made of hard cartilage and is used in defence! When threatened a Wombat may dive head first into its burrow, blocking the tunnel with its hardened rump and preventing predators from getting inside or latching onto them.

Geographic range: Endemic to South-eastern Australia.

Conservation status: Least concern.

Population Trend: Stable.

Threats: Appear to be no major threats to the species.

Common Emu (Dromaius Novaehollandiae)

After the Ostrich, the Emu is the second largest bird in the world by height. Emus have three toes on each foot which is an adaptation for running. They are incredibly fast and can reach speeds of up to 30mph. They are good swimmers and can also jump at vertical heights of up to two metres. Emus routinely swallow small stones which stay in their gizzard, helping them to grind up food.

Geographic Range: Distributed throughout mainland Australia.

Conservation Status: Least Concern.

Population Trend: Stable.

Threats: No major threats to the species.

Dingy Skipper (Erynnis Tages)

Mainly a springtime and early summer Butterfly, with sightings generally occurring between April and June. Also, occasionally sighted in July and August. Lives in close knit colonies with the caterpillars feeding on common and Greater-bird's-foot Trefoil and Horseshoe Vetch

Geographic range: Widespread across Europe and Asia and locally distributed across Britain and Ireland. It has strongholds in central and southern England.

Conservation status: UK population has declined dramatically in recent years.

Threats: Improvement of grassland for agriculture which results in loss of suitable foodplants, Decline in traditional woodland management techniques such as coppicing, 'Tidying up' of wasteland and countryside in general and Human development on suitable habitat.

Faint-banded Sea Snake (Hydrophis Belcheri)

One of the world's most venomous snakes. It is reputed that a single bite of their venom may have enough potency to kill several adult humans. They are very timid and will not bite unless extremely provoked. Excellent swimmers, they use their paddle like tail for efficiency. They can hold their breath underwater for over seven hours.

Geographic Range: Resident in Cambodia, Indonesia, Malaysia, Papua New Guinea, The Philippines, Singapore, Thailand and Vietnam.

Conservation Status: Data Deficient.

Population Trend: Unknown.

Threats: Predated on by sharks, moray eels and humans, Fishing and harvesting of aquatic resources (getting caught as bycatch in trawls).

Greater Horseshoe Bat (Rhinolophus Ferrumequinum)

One of Europe's largest Bat species, easily distinguished by the large horseshoe shaped nose which is used as part of their echolocation system. Females form maternity colonies during breeding season that typically can comprise up to 200 individuals. They hang in the classic upside down pose, cloaking themselves with their wings. During hibernation, they tend to roost in caves, tunnels and abandoned mines although they can also be found in old buildings, barns and churches. They have a lifespan of up to 30 years.

Geographic Range: Found in the UK and across Southern Europe into the Middle East and onwards through the Himalaya into China. Also resident in Japan and in the north of Algeria, Tunisia and Morocco.

Conservation Status: Least Concern.

Population Trend: Decreasing.

Threats: Human intrusions and disturbances, Pollution from agricultural pesticides reducing prey abundance, and Loss of roost sites and foraging areas.

Heath Monitor (Varanus Rosenbergi)

This species has adapted well to cooler climates and is the most cold tolerant Monitor Lizard in Australia. They are active predators but will also scavenge and eat carrion. Solitary except during courtship and breeding season, they use hollow logs, rock crevices or animal burrows to hide and rest. Females lay their eggs into termite nests which provide the perfect temperature for incubation. Also, once the young hatch, they have a ready source of available termite food.

Geographic Range: Southern parts of Australia below 30 degree south latitude (South Australia, Western Australia, Victoria, Australian Capital Territory, New South Wales).

Conservation Status: Least Concern.

Population Trend: Unknown.

Threats: Invasive species, genes and diseases, Removal of termite mounds, Clearance of habitat and vehicle collisions.

Kea (Nestor Notabilis)

The Kea is a highly intelligent species. Individuals have been documented using tools and others have been trained to move items in an itemised order to receive treats. They are polygamous. One male may mate with up to four females, who will build their nests on the ground in rock crevasses, holes or under logs. They have a high mortality rate with only 27% of Kea chicks living for longer than a year. Keas are omnivores and eat a variety of plant species as well as Beetle Larvae and baby birds. They may also scavenge on animal carcasses such as deer and sheep.

Geographic Range: Found on New Zealand's South Island.

Conservation Status: Endangered.

Population Trend: Decreasing.

Threats: Livestock farming, Hunting and trapping, Human intrusions and disturbances, Invasive species, Climate change and severe weather.

Leopard Cat (Prionailurus Bengalensis)

About the size of a large domestic cat. Solitary, usually hunting at night, they generally spend daylight hours resting in trees. They have excellent climbing and swimming abilities. Female Leopard Cats are known as *Queens*.

Geographic Range: Widespread throughout many parts of Asia including the islands of Borneo, Sumatra and Java.

Conservation status: Least Concern.

Population Trend: Stable.

Threats: Residential and Commercial Development, Logging and timber harvesting, Fragmentation of habitat, Hunting and trapping.

Leopard Seal (Hydrurga Leptonyx)

Leopard Seals are enormous. They can reach weights of up to 590kg and grow up to three metres in length. However, despite this size they have a streamlined shape with large fore flippers. This allows them to propel through the water at high speed. They are extremely efficient predators and feed on a variety of food such as squidfish and birds. They can even filter Krill through their teeth, which makes up a high percentage of their diet. They are exceptionally solitary but produce loud vocalisations under water. It is thought that these acoustic communications help them to find and select mates. They are known to live up to 26 years in the wild. Orcas are their only recognised predator.

Geographic Range: Found in Antarctic and Sub-Antarctic waters including Australia, French Southern Territories, Heard Island and McDonald Islands, South Georgia, Brazil, Chile, The Cook Islands, Falkland Islands, New Zealand, Saint Helena, Ascension and South Africa.

Conservation Status: Least Concern.

Population Trend: Unknown.

Threats: Fishing and harvesting of aquatic resources, Human intrusions and disturbances, Climate change and severe weather and reducing abundance of prey.

Little Penguin (Eudyptula Minor)

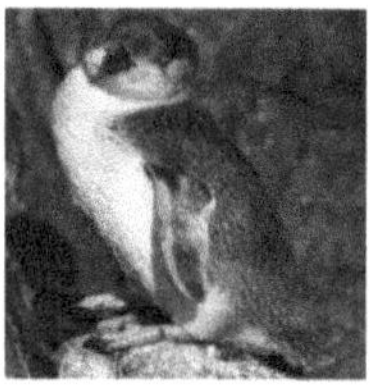

The smallest of the world's Penguin species, also known as the Fairy Penguin. They are the only Penguins to breed in Australia. Their feathers are kept waterproof by preening regularly whilst utilising a special gland above the tail to rub tiny drops of oil onto them.

Geographic range: Australia (New South Wales, South Australia, Tasmania, Victoria, Western Australia) and New Zealand.

Conservation status: Least concern.

Population Trend: Stable.

Threats: Residential and commercial development, Agriculture and aquaculture, Oil and gas drilling, Human intrusions and disturbance.

Pollution, Climate change and severe weather.

Little Red Flying Fox (Pteropus Scapulatus)

Highly nomadic, they move regularly between coastal rainforests and dry inland regions in search of prime feeding areas that are abundant with flowers and fruits. Well-developed vision and smell helps in detecting food and the eucalyptus blossom can make up large proportions of their diet. They benefit ecosystems through pollinating and dispersing seeds of the plants which they consume. They are a highly social species that gather in large groups known as camps, some of which can contain up to a million individuals. Tree branches have been known to break under the weight of their enormous numbers. They are excellent climbers and use their feet and webbed thumbs to grip onto tree branches.

Geographic range: Widespread across Northern And Eastern Australia and also occurs on various islands in the Torres Strait. Vagrant sightings occasionally in South Australia and New Zealand.

Conservation Status: Least Concern.

Population Trend: Unknown.

Threats: No known major threats to the species although local populations are sometimes threatened by loss or modification of feeding habitat due to agriculture.

Long-nosed Potoroo (Potorous Tridactylus)

Potoroos are marsupials. Young only weigh 0.3 grams when born and stay in their mothers pouch for four to five months. When they leave the pouch they remain near their mother to continue feeding from her for another 40 days or so. Once weaned, they branch out on their own and remain mostly solitary. Potoroos inhabit the dense understorey of forests where they feed on fungi which forms a large proportion of their diet. They also eat seeds, tubers, fruits and vegetation. They are mainly nocturnal and will rest up during the day in a leaf nest in dense cover. Females carry nesting materials with their semi-prehensile tail.

Geographic Range: Patchy distribution across parts of Australia (Victoria, Tasmania, South Australia, Queensland and New South Wales).

Conservation Status: Near Threatened.

Population Trend: Decreasing.

Threats: Loss and fragmentation of habitat due to residential and commercial development as well as logging and wood harvesting and Predation by non-native species such as foxes and domestic cats.

Manx Shearwater (Puffinus Puffinus)

A Shearwater can soar with maximum efficiency due to the placement of its long slender wings. This enables them to cover vast distances and it has been estimated that long lived individuals will have clocked over a million miles across their lifetime. They fly low above the ocean surface in daylight as they search for food and will feed on Fish, Shrimp, Squid and small marine organisms. They can dive to a depth of 30 metres in search of this prey and their tube shaped nostrils help them to excrete the salt from the seawater. By night, they return under cover of darkness to feed their solitary chick. This offers them protection from potential attack by large birds such as Black-backed Gulls.

Geographic Range: Breeds in the North Atlantic with sizable colonies in the UK and Ireland. Additional breeding sites are found in Iceland, the USA, Canada, The Azores and Canary Islands. Expands its range in the winter months to the Atlantic coast of South America and the west coast of South Africa.

Conservation Status: Least Concern.

Population Trend: Unknown.

Threats: Predation of eggs and chicks and Marine pollution.

Northern Gannet (Morus Bassanus)

Northern Gannets are the largest native seabird found along the coasts of the Atlantic Ocean. They are awkward on land and walk with difficult. Sometimes they may have trouble getting airborne from flat areas. However, they are fast and powerful fliers and are also incredibly streamlined for diving. They use their wings and tail to control the direction of their dives and will fold their wings tight against their body just before impact. This powerful entry enables penetration up to eleven metres underwater and they have been known to swim down to depths of 25 metres and beyond. They feed mainly on fish such as Sardines, Haddock, Smelt and Atlantic Cod as well as other shoal forming species.

Geographic Range: Found on both sides of the Atlantic Ocean. Prominent breeding sites include France, the United Kingdom, Ireland, Iceland, Norway and Eastern Canada.

Conservation Status: Least Concern.

Population Trend: Increasing.

Threats: Fishing and harvesting of aquatic resources and Marine Pollution.

Orca (Orcinus Orca)

Commonly called Killer Whales because of their renowned hunting ability. They sometimes work in pods of up to 40 individuals, to chase larger animals, such as Whales Sharks. They are most likely the second most wide ranging mammal on the planet (after humans). Orcas can't fully sleep as they have to come to the surface to breathe. To combat this, they sleep with one half of their brain at a time. This means that when the left side of their brain is asleep the right eye is open and vice versa.

Geographic Range: Occur in all oceans from Antarctic to Arctic regions and in tropical and partly enclosed seas.

Conservation Status: Data deficient.

Population Trend: Unknown.

Threats: Oil and gas drilling, Disturbance from shipping lanes, Overfishing and harvesting of aquatic resources, Pollution, Human intrusions and disturbance and Climate change and severe weather.

Pine Marten (Martes Martes)

Pine Martens are omnivores with a broad diet including Voles and Mice, Squirrels, small birds, eggs, berries and insects. They are incredible agile creatures, spending the majority of their time in trees. They can leap large distances between tree branches. As solitary creatures, that occupy large territories, they position their droppings (scat) in prominent locations to signal their presence to other martens. They are mostly active in twilight hours and at night so spend the day resting up in secretive locations. Their average lifespan is twelve years.

Geographic Range: Distributed across most of Europe and is also found in westernmost parts of Asian Russia, Kazakhstan and Northern Iran.

Conservation Status: Least Concern.

Population Trend: Stable.

Threats: Hunting and trapping and Habitat Fragmentation.

Platypus (Ornithorhynchus Anatinus)

Male Platypus have a secret weapon to use against predators. They have a spur on their hind feet which connects to a venom secreting gland. A strike from this spur can be enough to kill a dog.

Geographical Range: Endemic to Australia (Victoria, Tasmania, South Australia, Queensland, New South Wales).

Conservation Status: Near Threatened.

Population Trend: Decreasing.

Threats: Residential and commercial development, Agriculture and aquaculture, Pollution, Invasive species, Climate change and severe weather.

Privet Hawkmoth (Sphinx Ligustri)

The largest Hawkmoth resident in the UK. It flies at night and is attracted to light. The caterpillar is bright green, with a curved black tail and white and purple stripes along its body length. It pupates underground throughout winter and the adult moth flies between June and July. It feeds on the nectar of strongly scented flowers such as honeysuckle. Can be found in a variety of habitat from open woodland, gardens and hedgerows to coastal scrub.

Geographic Range: Can be found in England, Wales and Scotland but is more common in the Southern half of Britain.

Conservation Status: UK population considered to be stable.

UK distribution: Widespread and common across Southern Britain. Rarer and more patchily distributed in the North.

Threats: Loss of caterpillar food plants due to ash dieback disease.

Proboscis Monkey (Nasalis Larvatus)

Proboscis Monkeys are efficient swimmers due to their long limbs and webbed toes and can cover up to 20 metres underwater at a time. The massive male noses are thought to attract females as the loud bellows that they amplify through them act as alarm signals. The larger the nose, the more protection they can offer!

Geographic Range: Endemic to Borneo, occurring in Brunei, Indonesia (Kalimantan) and Malaysia (Sarawak and Sabah).

Conservation Status: Endangered.

Population Trend: Decreasing.

Threats: Residential and Commercial Development, Logging and timber harvesting, Hunting and trapping.

Red Deer (Cervus Elaphus)

Red Deer are highly social animals, living in large herds throughout the year. They graze predominantly on grasses and sedges and as ruminants, will regurgitate their food to chew it again. This aids the digestion process. They are a polygynous species with one male mating with multiple females. During rutting season the males compete vigorously to establish mating rights and dominant stags can maintain control over large harems. They are finely tuned animals with heightened senses of smell and hearing and over 300 degree field of vision. They can run at speeds of up to 70kph. They have evolved with all of these attributes to help them avoid predation. Their life span can be up to twenty years.

Geographic Range: Distributed across Europe and into North Africa and the Middle East.

Conservation Status: Least Concern.

Population Trend: Increasing.

Threats: Residential and commercial development, Livestock farming and ranching, Hunting and trapping, Human intrusions and disturbances and Invasive species.

Rhinoceros Hornbill (Buceros Rhinoceros)

These are monogamous birds with male and female forming close knit bonds for life. Occasionally they may form small flocks, however when this happens, the male continuously brings food to the female to maintain their pair bond. They make their nests inside hollow tree trunks and once the eggs are laid the female stays inside. The pair then pack mud over the tree cavity leaving only enough space for the male to pass food through. This offers protection for the female and her chicks. Rhinoceros Hornbill enjoy sunbathing and often perch facing towards the sun with their wings spread.

Geographic Range: Resident in Brunei Darussalem, Indonesia, Malaysia and Thailand.

Conservation Status: Vulnerable.

Population Trend: Decreasing.

Threats: Forest destruction through commercial and illegal logging, Hunting and trapping.

Sun Bear (Helarctos Malayanus)

Known affectionately as the Honey Bear for its love of honeycomb and honey. They utilise their exceptionally long tongues to reach into the bee hives to extract this precious nectar. Sun Bears are solitary animals and are excellent climbers. Sometimes they sleep in tree branches high above ground although they also utilise hollow logs and tree cavities as resting areas. They do not hibernate as the tropical region in which they live offers year round food supply. During mating season they show a range of behaviours such as mock fighting, head bobbing and hugging their mate. They are active during the day and night.

Geographic Range: Resident in Bangladesh, Brunei Darussalam, Cambodia, India, Indonesia, Laos (People's Democratic Republic), Malaysia, Myanmar, and Thailand.

Conservation Status: Vulnerable.

Population Trend: Decreasing.

Threats: Forest destruction through commercial and illegal logging, Fragmentation of habitat, Hunting and trapping.

Superb Lyrebird (Menura Novaehollandiae)

Lyrebirds spend most of the day on the forest floor, scratching in the leaf litter to find insects. If disturbed, they run fast through the undergrowth, sometimes emitting a loud alarm call. They generally roost in trees at night. Their name comes from the resemblance of their tail feather to the lyre, an ancient Greek musical instrument. 80% of their calls are mimics of other species or man made noises, however they also have their own calls which include whistles, cackling and shrieks.

Geographic Range: Australia (Extreme S/E Queensland, NSW, ACT and Victoria. They also have been introduced to Tasmania, although they are regarded as a Feral species there).

Conservation status: Least Concern.

Population Trend: Decreasing.

Threats: Climate Change and severe weather.

Tasmanian Devil (Sarcophilus Harrisii)

Devils have varied vocalisations which they use to scare off other animals and to avoid confrontations. These range from growls, coughs and snorts to sniffs, screeches and sneezes. When European settlers heard these sounds, they imagined they were surrounded by demons in the wilderness which is how the devil got its name. Devils store fat in their tails and a plump tail is the sign of good health. They have incredibly powerful jaws and ingest all parts of carrion and prey, including bones and fur. They've even been known to fall asleep inside rotten carcasses so they can continue feeding as soon as they wake up.

Geographic range: Found throughout mainland Tasmania. Reintroductions are also currently taking place of captive bred devils into large fenced off areas near Barrington Tops National Park on the Australian mainland.

Conservation status: Endangered.

Population trend: Decreasing.

Threats: Hunting and Trapping.

Devil Facial Tumour Disease, Dog kills and road kill

Tasmanian Pademelon (Thylogale Billardierii)

There are seven species of Pademelon in total, all native to Australia and Papua New Guinea. They are usually a solitary animal but come together on occasion to graze or mate. They tend to make their home in dense thickets of bush or scrub although they can also be found in forests and swampy habitats. A Pademelon can weigh up to 12kgs and typically range from 42 to 52 centimetres in height. Similar to Rabbits, Pademelons thump the ground with their hind legs to alert others of danger. The Tasmanian Pademelon has been known to eat nectar bearing flowers as well as its staple diet of grasses, leaves, herbs and berries.

Geographic Range: Found on the island of Tasmania and some of the larger islands of the Bass Strait.

Conservation Status: Least Concern.

Population Trend: Stable.

Threats: Invasive species such as Foxes, Attacks from dogs.

Wedge-tailed Eagle (Aquila Audax)

With a wingspan which can reach over two metres, they are one of the world's largest Eagle. Pairs are quite territorial and are monogamous, staying together for life. They generally make a number of huge nests, in prominent positions across their territory. This offers the opportunity to utilise different nest locations from year to year. Individual nests can be as large as two metres across and three metres deep and smaller birds such as Finches often make their nest in their underside. Through this, they are utilising the Eagle's presence to gain protection from other predators. Wedge-tailed Eagles can soar at altitudes up to 2,000 metres.

Geographic Range: Breeding Populations across Australia, Indonesia and Papua New Guinea.

Conservation Status: Least Concern.

Population Trend: Increasing.

Threats: Loss of nesting sites through tree clearance, Secondary poisoning, Collisions with vehicles, fences and overhead wires.

Whale Shark (Rhincodon Typus)

This is the world's largest fish and is known as the gentle giant of the ocean. Some grow up to 12 metres long. As filter feeders, they cannot bite or chew but consume Plankton as well as small Fish and Shrimp. They do this by stretching their mouth up to four feet wide. It is thought that they process up to 6000 litres of water through their gills every hour. Although Whale Sharks migrate over vast distances, they move at speeds of little more than three mph.

Geographic Range: Distributed across all temperate and tropical seas with the exception of the Mediterranean.

Conservation Status: Endangered.

Population Trend: Decreasing.

Threats: Oil and gas drilling, Disturbance from shipping lanes, Overfishing and harvesting of aquatic resources, Human intrusions and disturbances.

Yellow-eyed Penguin (Megadyptes Antipodes)

This is the least social of all Penguin species. Rather than living in colonies they prefer to live a more sedentary life, nesting in forests or bushes close to the seashore. They communicate with their mate and chicks through high pitched vocalisations. Their diet consists primarily of Fish and they spend large parts of their time feeding at sea. Yellow-eyed Penguins can dive to depths of 100m and are known to hold their breath for up to four minutes.

Geographic Range: This species is endemic to New Zealand. It is found in two distinct areas. The Northern population occupies the southeast coast of New Zealand's south island. The Southern population is found in the Subantarctic Auckland Islands and Campbell Island.

Conservation Status: Endangered.

Population Trend: Decreasing.

Threats: Degradation of habitat through agricultural development, Invasive species such as introduced predators, Human intrusions and disturbances around nesting areas, and Climate Change resulting in declines in the number of their prey population.

About the Author

Gerry O'Brien is a committed eco-therapist, dedicated Forest Ranger and all round wildlife enthusiast. He lives on the borderland of England and Wales, in the beautiful Wye Valley, with his daughter Aoife, their three Cats, Bella, Luna and Pixie and their Barn Owl, The Professor.

With his varied life experiences, personable nature and passionate disposition, Gerry is the perfect person to highlight nature's wonderful delights, through intimate guided tours or interactive talks and presentations. He can also be consulted for eco-therapy, mindfulness and well-being sessions.

As a first time author, he is keen to reach out and connect to as many people as possible and to help in some way in bringing the delights of the natural world back into the forefront of our minds.

He is presently working on a follow up to *'Wildlife Whispers'* which will provide intimate detail on his wonderful experiences over the last twelve years with his Barn Owl companion.

Gerry can be contacted:
email: info@gerryobrienconsultancy.com
Instagram and Facebook pages @gerrytheranger
and website: www.gerryobrienconsultancy.com

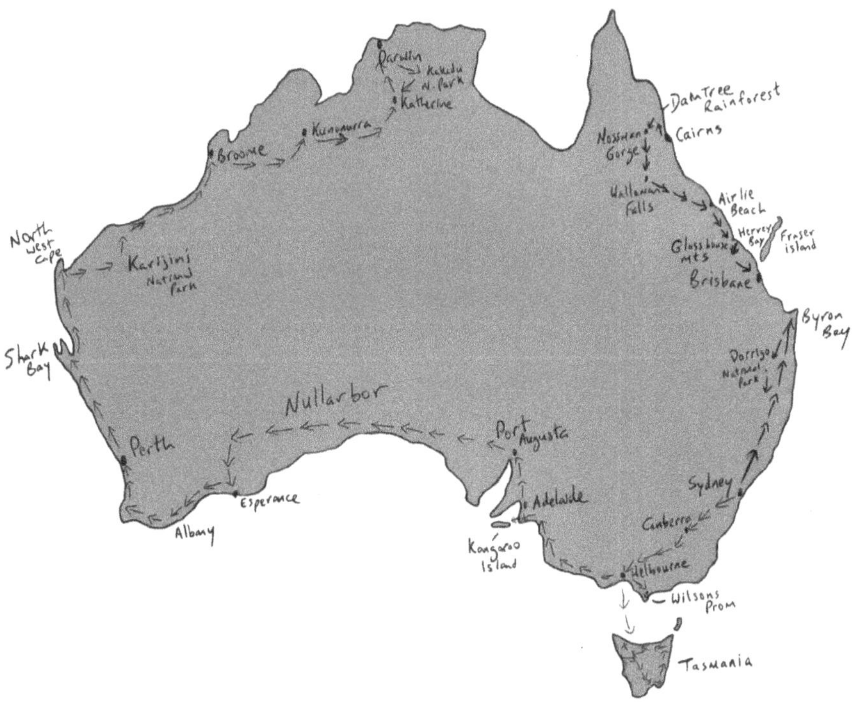

Australian Routes

References

Books

Barkham, Patrick, *The Butterfly Isles: A Summer in Search of Our Emperors and Admirals*, (Granta), 2011

Bryson, Bill. *Down Under*, (Black Swan) 2010

Holden, Phil and Cleeves, Tim, *RSPB Handbook of British Birds* (4th Edition), (Bloomsbury), 2014

Hutton, Mary, *Free the Bears: How an ordinary Perth Grandmother became an Extraordinary Animal Activist*, (MacMillan), 2010

King, Stephen, *On Writing: A Memoir of The Craft*, (20th Anniversary Edition), (Hodder & Stoughton), 2020

Moon, Ron, and Moon, Viv, *National Parks Australia: Enjoy the Beauty of Australia's Natural Heritage* (2nd Edition), (Gregorys), 2006

Nightengale, Neil, Clevers, Jeni, Pearson, Hugh and Summerhill, Mary, *Wild Down Under: The Natural History of Australasia*, (BBC Books), 2003

Parry, James, *The National Forest: Heritage in the Making*, (The National Forest Company), 2006

Sterry, Paul, *Complete Irish Wildlife*, (Harper Collins) 2004

Sterry, Paul, *Collins Complete British Animals: A Photographic Guide to Every Common Species*, (Harper Collins), 2005

Thomas, Jeremy and Lewington, Richard, *The Butterflies of Britain & Ireland*, (British Wildlife), 2010

Websites

Animal Facts, The, *Emu Fact File*, https://www.theanimalfacts.com/birds/emu 16/09/2021

Animal Facts, The, *Kea Fact File*, https://www.theanimalfacts.com/birds/kea 25/10/2021

Animal Facts, The, *Heath Goanna Fact File*, https://www.theanimalfacts.com/reptiles/heath-goanna 08/09/2021

Animal Facts, The, *Superb Lyrebird Fact File*, https://www.theanimalfacts.com/birds/superb-lyrebird 13/06/2021

Animalia, *Australian Sea Lion*, https://animalia.bio/leopard-cat 09/09/2021

Animalia, *Leopard Cat*, https://animalia.bio/leopard-cat 13/06/2021

Animalia, *Little Red Flying Fox*, https://animalia.bio/little-red-flying-fox 20/09/2021

Animalia, *Northern Gannet*, https://animalia.bio/northern-gannet 14/10/2021

Animalia, *Proboscis Monkey*, https://animalia.bio/proboscis-monkey 13/06/2021

Animalia, *Red Deer*, https://animalia.bio/red-deer 08/04/2021

Animalia, *Rhinocerous Hornbill*, https://animalia.bio/rhinoceros-hornbill 19/10/2021

Animalia, *Sun Bear*, https://animalia.bio/sun-bear 19/10/2021

Animalia, *Yellow-Eyed Penguin*, https://animalia.bio/yellow-eyed-penguin 26/10/2021

Australian Museum, *Australian Brush Turkey*, https://australian.museum/learn/animals/birds/australian-brush-turkey 18/10/2021

Australian Museum, *Australian Bustard*, https://australian.museum/learn/animals/birds/australian-bustard 19/09/2021

AZ Animals, *Pademelon*, https://a-z-animals.com/animals/pademelon 16/06/2021

BBC, *Blue Planet*, https://www.bbc.co.uk/programmes/p04tjbtx 06/08/2021

Birdlife Australia, *Comb-crested Jacana*, https://www.birdlife.org.au/bird-profile/comb-crested-jacana 27/09/2021

Bush Heritage Australia, *Wedge-tailed Eagles*, https://www.bushheritage.org.au/species/wedge-tailed-eagles 10/09/2021

Butterfly Conservation, *Dingy Skipper*, https://butterfly-conservation.org/butterflies/dingy-skipper 01/12/2021

Butterfly Conservation, *Privet Hawk-moth*, https://butterfly-conservation.org/moths/privet-hawk-moth 01/12/2021

Critter Man, *The Faint-Banded (Or Belcher's) Sea Snake*, https://critter.science/the-faint-banded-or-belchers-sea-snake 27/09/2021

Doogue, Geraldine, *Lyre Birds Feral in Tasmania*, https://www.abc.net.au/radionational/programs/saturdayextra/lyre-birds-feral-in-tasmania/3449828 12/06/2021

Editorial Team Oyster, *14 Intriguing Facts About Borneo*, https://www.oysterworldwide.com/news/14-intriguing-facts-about-borneo 14/12/2021

Fact Animal, *Killer Whale Facts*, https://factanimal.com/killer-whale 16/09/2021

IUCN Red List, *Australian Sea Lion*, https://www.iucnredlist.org/species/14549/45228341 08/09/2021

IUCN Red List, *Bornean Orangutan*, https://www.iucnredlist.org/species/17975/123809220 11/06/2021

IUCN Red List, *Comb-crested Jacana*, https://www.iucnredlist.org/species/22693540/93411572 27/09/2021

IUCN Red List, *Common Emu*, https://www.iucnredlist.org/species/22678117/131902466 16/09/2021

IUCN Red List, *Common Wombat*, https://www.iucnredlist.org/species/40556/21958985 12/06/2021

IUCN Red List, *Faint-banded Sea Snake*, https://www.iucnredlist.org/species/176751/7297371 27/09/2021

IUCN Red List, *Greater Horseshoe Bat*, https://www.iucnredlist.org/species/19517/8947877 09/12/2021

IUCN Red List, *Heath Monitor*, https://www.iucnredlist.org/species/178031/101744611 08/09/2021

IUCN Red List, *Kea*, https://www.iucnredlist.org/species/22684831/119243358 25/10/2021

IUCN Red List, *Killer Whale*, https://www.iucnredlist.org/species/15421/50368125 16/09/2021

IUCN Red List, *Leopard Cat*, https://www.iucnredlist.org/species/18146/50661611 11/06/2021

IUCN Red List, *Leopard Seal*, https://www.iucnredlist.org/species/10340/45226422 25/10/2021

IUCN Red List, *Little Penguin*, https://www.iucnredlist.org/species/22697805/202126091 12/06/2021

IUCN Red List, *Little Red Flying Fox*, https://www.iucnredlist.org/species/18758/22087637 16/09/2021

IUCN Red List, *Long-nosed Potoroo*, https://www.iucnredlist.org/species/41511/166499137 28/09/2021

IUCN Red List, *Manx Shearwater*, https://www.iucnredlist.org/species/22698226/166330248 09/12/2021

IUCN Red List, *Northern Gannet*, https://www.iucnredlist.org/species/22696657/166314602 11/10/2021

IUCN Red List, *Pine Marten*, https://www.iucnredlist.org/species/12848/45199169 02/12/2021

IUCN Red List, *Platypus*, https://www.iucnredlist.org/species/40488/21964009 12/06/2021

IUCN Red List, *Proboscis Monkey*, https://www.iucnredlist.org/species/14352/195372486 11/06/2021

IUCN Red List, *Red Deer*, https://www.iucnredlist.org/species/55997072/142404453 30/11/2021

IUCN Red List, *Red-Necked Wallaby*, https://www.iucnredlist.org/species/40566/21953329 16/06/2021

IUCN Red List, *Rhinocerous Hornbill*, https://www.iucnredlist.org/species/22682450/184960407 15/10/2021

IUCN Red List, *Saltwater Crocodile*, https://www.iucnredlist.org/species/5668/3047556 16/09/2021

IUCN Red List, *Sun Bear*, https://www.iucnredlist.org/species/9760/123798233 15/10/2021

IUCN Red List, *Superb Lyrebird*, https://www.iucnredlist.org/species/22703605/132071218 12/06/2021

IUCN Red List, *Tasmanian Devil*, https://www.iucnredlist.org/species/40540/10331066 13/06/2021

IUCN Red List, *Tasmanian Pademelon*, https://www.iucnredlist.org/species/40571/21958627 16/06/2021

IUCN Red List, *Wedge-tailed Eagle*, https://www.iucnredlist.org/species/22696064/93542539 10/09/2021

IUCN Red List, *Whale Shark*, https://www.iucnredlist.org/species/19488/2365291 16/09/2021

IUCN Red List, *Yellow-eyed Penguin*, https://www.iucnredlist.org/species/22697800/182703046 25/10/2021

Kidadl, *Fun Australia Bustard Facts for Kids*, https://kidadl.com/facts/animals/australian-bustard-facts 19/09/2021

Kidadl, *Fun Greater Horseshoe Bat Facts for Kids*, https://kidadl.com/facts/animals/greater-horseshoe-bat-facts 09/12/2021

Kiddle, Little Penguin Facts for Kids, https://kids.kiddle.co/Little_penguin 13/06/2021

Lewis, Amy, (2021) *UK Hawk-moth identification and facts*, https://www.woodlandtrust.org.uk/blog/2021/06/hawk-moth-identification 01/12/2021

Live Science, *Platypus Facts*, https://www.livescience.com/27572-platypus.html 12/06/2021

Mammal Age, *Spotted-tail Quoll*, https://www.mammalage.com/spotted-tail-quoll 13/06/2021

National Museum Australia, *Extinction of Thylacine*, https://www.nma.gov.au/defining-moments/resources/extinction-of-thylacine 13/06/2021

National Ocean Service, *What's the Difference between Seals and Sea Lions*, https://oceanservice.noaa.gov/facts/seal-sealion.html 09/09/2021

Oceanwide Expeditions, *Danger Beneath the Water*, https://oceanwide-expeditions.com/blog/danger-beneath-the-water-10-facts-about-leopard-seals 26/10/2021

Parks and Wildlife Service, (Shark Bay World Heritage), *Monkey Mia*, https://www.sharkbay.org/place/monkey-mia 18/11/2021

People's Trust For Endangered Species, *Pine Marten*, https://ptes.org/get-informed/facts-figures/pine-marten 02/12/2021

Rural Sprout, *Rewild Your Garden: 10 Easy Things You Can Do To Make A Big Difference*, https://www.ruralsprout.com/rewild-your-garden 13/01/2021

Scotland's Nature, *Species of the Month*, https://scotlandsnature.blog/2016/05/02/species-of-the-month-the-manx-shearwater-the-charming-frequent-flier 09/12/2021

Smithsonian's National Zoo and Conservation Biology Institute, *Bennett's Wallaby*, https://nationalzoo.si.edu/animals/bennetts-wallaby 16/06/2021

Stringer, A., MacPherson, J., Carter, S., Gill, R., Ambrose-Oji, B., Wilson, R., Kelsall, P., Fern, W., Galbraith, L., Hilario, C.,Parry, G. and Taylor, A. *The feasibility of reintroducing pine martens to the Forest of Dean and lower Wye Valley*, https://www.researchgate.net/publication/337604680_The_feasibility_of_reintroducing_pine_martens_to_the_Forest_of_Dean_and_lower_Wye_Valley 02/12/2021

Spencer, Joanne, *Manx Shearwater Bird*, https://animalcorner.org/animals/manx-shearwater-bird 09/09/2021

Van der Pol, Marika, *Fast Facts on Long-nosed Potoroos*, https://www.conservationecologycentre.org/2013/01/21/fast-facts-on-long-nosed-potoroos/#:~:text=%20Fast%20Facts%20on%20Long-nosed%20Potoroos%20%201,forests%20are%20important...%205%20Weight%3A%20660-1600g%20More%20 30/09/2021

Watson, Sophia, *Fun Facts About Tasmanian Devils*, https://www.australia.com/en/things-to-do/wildlife/tasmanian-devil-facts.html#:~:text=Fun%20facts%20about%20Tasmanian%20Devils%201%20THEY%20HAVE,teeth%20are%20unique%21%20...%2010%20THEY%20ARE%20ENDANGERED 13/06/2021

Wikipedia contributors, *Australian Bustard*, (Wikipedia, The Free Encyclopedia), https://en.wikipedia.org/wiki/Australian_bustard 6/8/2022

Wikipedia contributors, *Australian Sea Lion*, (Wikipedia, The Free Encyclopedia), https://en.wikipedia.org/wiki/Australian_sea_lion 6/8/2022

Wikipedia contributors, *Bornean Orangutan*, (Wikipedia, The Free Encyclopedia), https://en.wikipedia.org/wiki/Bornean_orangutan 6/8/2022

Wikipedia contributors, *Comb-crested Jacana*, (Wikipedia, The Free Encyclopedia), https://en.wikipedia.org/wiki/Comb-crested_jacana 6/8/2022

Wikipedia contributors, *Emu*, (Wikipedia, The Free Encyclopedia), https://en.wikipedia.org/wiki/Emu 6/8/2022

Wikipedia contributors, *Faint-banded Sea Snake*, (Wikipedia, The Free Encyclopedia), https://en.wikipedia.org/wiki/Hydrophis_belcheri 6/8/2022

Wikipedia contributors, *Heath Monitor*, (Wikipedia, The Free Encyclopedia), https://en.wikipedia.org/wiki/Rosenberg%27s_monitor 6/8/2022

Wikipedia contributors, *Leopard Cat*, (Wikipedia, The Free Encyclopedia), https://en.wikipedia.org/wiki/Leopard_cat 6/8/2022

Wikipedia contributors, *Leopard Seal*, (Wikipedia, The Free Encyclopedia), https://en.wikipedia.org/wiki/Leopard_seal 6/8/2022

Wikipedia contributors, *Little Red Flying Fox*, (Wikipedia, The Free Encyclopedia), https://en.wikipedia.org/wiki/Little_red_flying_fox 6/8/2022

Wikipedia contributors, *Little Penguin*, (Wikipedia, The Free Encyclopedia), https://en.wikipedia.org/wiki/Little_penguin 6/8/2022

Wikipedia contributors, *Long-nosed Potoroo*, (Wikipedia, The Free Encyclopedia), https://en.wikipedia.org/wiki/Long-nosed_potoroo 6/8/2022

Wikipedia contributors, *Northern Gannet*, (Wikipedia, The Free Encyclopedia), https://en.wikipedia.org/wiki/Northern_gannet 6/8/2022

Wikipedia contributors, *Orca*, (Wikipedia, The Free Encyclopedia), https://en.wikipedia.org/wiki/Orca 6/8/2022

Wikipedia contributors, *European Pine Marten*, (Wikipedia, The Free Encyclopedia), https://en.wikipedia.org/wiki/European_pine_marten 6/8/2022

Wikipedia contributors, *Platypus*, (Wikipedia, The Free Encyclopedia), https://en.wikipedia.org/wiki/Platypus 6/8/2022

Wikipedia contributors, *Proboscis Monkey*, (Wikipedia, The Free Encyclopedia), https://en.wikipedia.org/wiki/Proboscis_monkey 6/8/2022

Wikipedia contributors, *Rhinoceros Hornbill*, (Wikipedia, The Free Encyclopedia), https://en.wikipedia.org/wiki/Rhinoceros_hornbill 6/8/2022

Wikipedia contributors, *Superb Lyrebird*, (Wikipedia, The Free Encyclopedia), https://en.wikipedia.org/wiki/Superb_lyrebird 6/8/2022

Wikipedia contributors, *Tasmanian Devil*, (Wikipedia, The Free Encyclopedia), https://en.wikipedia.org/wiki/Tasmanian_devil 6/8/2022

Wikipedia contributors, *Tasmanian Pademelon*, (Wikipedia, The Free Encyclopedia), https://en.wikipedia.org/wiki/Tasmanian_pademelon 6/8/2022

Wikipedia contributors, *Wedge-tailed Eagle*, (Wikipedia, The Free Encyclopedia), https://en.wikipedia.org/wiki/Wedge-tailed_eagle 6/8/2022

Wildlife Trust, The, *Muntjac Deer*, (Wikipedia, The Free Encyclopedia), https://www.wildlifetrusts.org/wildlife-explorer/mammals/muntjac-deer 01/12/2021

Wired, *The Creature Feature: 10 Fun Facts About Wombats*, https://www.wired.com/2014/12/creature-feature-10-fun-facts-wombats 13/06/2021

World Wildlife Fund, *Dugong*, https://www.worldwildlife.org/species/dugong 18/11/2021

WWF-UK, *Top 10 Facts About Orangutans*, https://www.wwf.org.uk/learn/fascinating-facts/orangutans 13/06/2021

WWF-UK, *Top 5 Facts About Whale Sharks*, https://www.wwf.org.uk/learn/fascinating-facts/whale-sharks 16/09/2021

Films

Apted, Michael, *Gorillas in the Mist*, Directed by Michael Apted (Universal Pictures), USA, 1988

Photographs

Bridges, Josie, *Radio Tracking Pine Martens*, Forest of Dean, UK, 2015

Brownlee, Derek, *Dingy Skipper*, Leicestershire, UK 2009

Kenny, Ian, Red Deer, Peak District National Park, UK, 2011

Phillip Island National Park, *Penguin Parade*, Phillip Island, Australia, 2019

Plant, Steve, *Privet Hawkmoth*, Leicestershire, UK, 2009

Priddis, David, *Greater Horseshoe Bat*, Forest of Dean, UK, 2019

Troman, Charlie, Gerry O'Brien holding his Barn Owl, *'The Professor'* on the back cover https://www.charlietroman.com

Wakelin, Abbie, Proboscis Monkey used to generate front cover illustration

All other photographs credited to Gerry O'Brien and Abigail Simpson

Illustrations

Animal and Bungle Bungles illustrations credited to Abigail Simpson

Map illustrations credited to the author, Gerry O'Brien

Acknowledgements

Mam and Dad - For providing the security, love and freedom that encouraged my childhood explorations.

Liam, Anne and **Patricia**, my brother and sisters - I wish I could see you all more often!

Abigail - for sharing the travel adventures with me. What a magical time in our lives!

Aoife - For all the fun and adventures that we share together! Thank you for motivating and inspiring me to be at my best.

My Cousins - Who shared many of those youthful adventures. They truly were halcyon days!

My Grand Uncle Tom - For instilling a love of folklore and legend.

Margaret McGrath, my teacher, - For sharing her love of the natural world in our classroom.

Mary Hutton, Matt Hunt, Steve Irwin and countless ecologists and wildlife rangers and guides - For inspiring me along the way.

My Uncle Tom, and all the family in Perth, - For looking after us so well. Can't wait to come and see you all again!

Ali Bannister - My cover design illustrator. Not only a wonderful artist but a truly incredible human being. Thank you deeply for all your support and guidance.

Jun Chow, my friend, healer and website guru - Thanks for all your guidance and support. It is much appreciated.

Ian Kenny, my friend - For sharing wild adventures with me and for the use of your wonderful Red Deer image.

David Priddis, Eric Palmer, Sarah Howells and **Laurent Duverge** - For all your advice and guidance regarding bats! I loved my time on the radio-tracking project with you. (A special thanks to David for the Greater Horseshoe Bat image and the text regarding their echolocation)

Brian Phillips and **Gloucestershire Bat Group** - For organising and implementing the hibernation roost counts. What an adventure! I felt like a character in Jules Verne '*Journey to the Center of the Earth*'.

Ken Orpe - For all your incredible enthusiasm for butterflies and for your generosity and good will regarding advice and use of images

Steve Plant and **Derek Brownlee** - For use of your Privet Hawkmoth and Dingy Skipper photographs.

Abbie Wakelin - For the generous use of your Proboscis Monkey image for our cover design

Holly Dowsett and all at **Phillip Island Nature Parks** - For the use of the beautiful Little Penguin image in Chapter 2 and for all the amazing conservation work that inspires so many.

Cat McNicol, Josie Bridges and all at **Project Pine Marten** and **Gloucestershire Wildlife Trust** - For your time, support and guidance. It's been great working alongside you all.

Andrew Stringer - For supporting me along the way.

Neil Hanshaw and my old **Ranger Team** in the **Goyt Valley** - I learned a lot from my time with you. Thank you so much!

Forest Holidays - For providing the opportunity to continue my Ranger journey and offering the perfect setting to enthuse and educate about wildlife.

Jess Robinson - For all your support, friendship and guidance.

Kate Rushworth - For being a shining light when times are dark. You always believe in me even when I lose all faith in myself. Thank you deeply for your support, guidance and friendship.

Charlie Troman For the generous use of the back cover photograph.

James Bastick and **David Meehan** - Old friends are the best. Thank you for always being there for me.

Anna Lee Galway and **Earl Smith** - My waffle buddies! Certainly helped pull us through lockdown. I miss our long chats since life has got so busy again! Thanks for all your support.

Gret Cairns - For always supporting and believing in me! Thank you for sharing the highs and lows along the way.

Rob Adsley - For your friendship and for helping pull me through our University assignments on those occasions when it was all getting too much!

My Ecotherapy Cohorts - What a journey we've all just shared! There's another book just waiting to be written about our phenomenal insights into the healing power of nature.

Salli-Anne Millward, my ranger buddy - For all your support and friendship. There have been some crazy days but we've had good laughs along the way!

Tom McCaughren - For creating wonderful stories that fired my imagination and added fuel to my wildlife passion. Also for your wonderful and generous foreword, I am deeply indebted.

Nick Spellman - For the wonderful gift that you bestowed on me! The Professor has brought a lot of magic into my life and is the nucleus for my next creative project.

Ed Drewitt and **Rosie Jones** - For all your support. Couldn't quite fit extracts about our toad patrols in, but maybe in Volume 2!

Ladey, Abbirose and **Denis Adey** - For being such a friendly, supportive and fabulous publishing team.

Debra Pitchford - For setting the wheels in motion! Much appreciated.

All Members at **The Book Academy (a bookclub on steroids!)** - For sharing our love of writing, reading and all things literary.

Geraldine Calcraft - For your time, support and insightful comments. You really are the best beta-reader! Thank you for taking the time to do so!

Charlie Taylor - For your support and guidance! What a wonderful journey; being an author.

Mike Bailey and all the team at **Hereford Bat Rescue** - I'm blown away by your passion, commitment and dedication to bats. What an inspiring team. You give me hope that all is not lost and have highlighted the value of collaborative work.

The Professor - My wonderful feathered companion, much gratitude for bringing a large sprinkling of joy into my life! I love how you light up everyone's day'

Finally... to all those I've interacted with over the years I've met so many amazing people. You've all helped to mould, inspire and shape my outlook on life. Thanks for sharing my journey even if only briefly. Apologies to anyone I may have forgotten to directly mention. It's not intentional but my oversight.

Thanks to You for reading my words.

Index

Index

A

O

P

Q

R

Your Notes

Your Notes

Your Notes

Your Notes

Your Notes

Endorsements

Gerry is one of those rare people with a heart that remains pure. A pure heart connects easily with nature. So, if you are longing for a deeper connection with the natural world and the joy for life that it brings, this extraordinary book is for you.

Patricia Gimenez-Salinas, Eco-therapist, Founder of Animatree

My two young boys and I have been lucky enough to spend several evenings wandering around the Forest of Dean with Gerry. Each time, he's managed to keep us entertained by pointing out things that are almost invisible to the naked eye. Marks on trees from wild boar, owl pellets, wild garlic. These rambles could go on for hours, with maybe a short break for some fresh nettle tea. My kids are ten and twelve and trust me, it takes something special to keep them entertained. Gerry has that something special. He has a real wonder and love for nature, and by treating young people as equals, he is able to communicate and share that respect for the great outdoors.

Iain Lee, British Broadcaster and Former Television Presenter

A celebration of the diversity of life on Earth. I was taken in by Gerry's down-to-earth writing style and how he makes the reader feel like a fellow traveller. This book is a timely reminder that life on Earth could hardly be any more magical than it already is. It is a delightfully easy read too.

Stephen McCabe, Author of The Moorfoot Tales: Lost Myths from Scotland

As our Forest Ranger at the Forest of Dean, Gerry is a trailblazing advocate for nature. He is a true wildlife enthusiast, taking action to restore biodiversity as well as doing everything in his power to raise both awareness and funds for environmental causes. As a company, we're fully supportive of Gerry's projects and we're excited to read all about his nature-fuelled journey and his encounters along the way.

Bruce McKendrick, Chief Executive Officer, Forest Holidays

Gerry has a unique ability to connect you to the beauty of nature. Follow his wonderful wildlife encounters across countries and continents. With vivid descriptions and beautiful illustration, it is a book you will return to again and again, lingering over the pages, drawn in by the passion Gerry has for all the natural world has to offer.

Debra Pitchford, Learning and Development Consultant

Gerry is one of a kind, his infectious energy makes him the perfect person to in-spire people of all ages about the beauty, wonder and importance of conserving the natural world. In person, he effortlessly connects people with nature and this book is a natural extension of this ability, his passion shines through on every page. You're there, living each adventure alongside him and it's impossible not to feel inspired to experience your own wildlife whispers.

Jess Robinson, Ecological Co-ordinator, Forest Holidays

This is a wonderful story of wildlife encounters and personal discoveries, told in a way that is captivating and engaging. Gerry's passion and respect for the natural world is truly inspiring and I am so pleased he listened to those '*whispers*' to take up a career in doing what he loves most. He is one of the best in the business to pass on wildlife learning and enthusiasm to the next generation and to give us hope for a healthy planet Earth.

Zoe Sewter, Access and Recreation Officer, The National Forest

Through his adventures on far-flung continents and his nature conservation work closer to home, Gerry O'Brien shares the story of a life well-lived and a deep appreciation for the natural world. *Wildlife Whispers*, is an antidote to the doom and gloom of the modern world. It is an invitation for us to connect to the wild that lies in and around us.

Kathryn Sheridan, Coach and Eco-therapist

Gerry brings the infinite diversity of the natural world into focus with this engaging retelling of his journey to a life dedicated to conservation. From fond recollections of being urinated on by primates to the joyful unpredictability of encounters with a whole host of exotic species including Quolls, Echidnas, Water Dragons and the improbably named Jesus Bird, this is a tale told by somebody with a genuine affinity and affection for all creatures. Despite the very real risks to wildlife across the globe, it's a mark of Gerry's attitude and approach that he chose to make this a hope-filled tale of the difference that dedicated individuals can make, an approach he has carried on in his own conservation work. It's a privilege to know Gerry and see his enthusiasm for his work, and a pleasure to recommend his expertise, enthusiasm and gentle, optimistic approach to all lovers of the natural world.

Martin Sweeney, Borderlands Outdoor Founder and Instructor

From the bog ponds of Ireland to the tropical rainforests of Borneo, *Wildlife Whispers* takes you on an immersive adventure with integrity and inspiration at its heart. Gerry's passion for conservation is second to none and his book reads like an intimate field guide with beautifully illustrated pictures throughout.

Charlotte L. Taylor, International Bestselling Author of the Broken Twigs series for Middle Grade Children and Co-founder of Wild Wood Press and Toadstool Tales.

WILDLIFE WHISPERS

GERRY O'BRIEN

CONSULTANCY

Milton Keynes UK
Ingram Content Group UK Ltd.
UKHW051019310124
436982UK00007B/161

9 781913 579456